Instruction/Answer Guide

YOU DECIDE!

Applying the Bill of Rights
to Real Cases

George Bundy Smith & Alene L. Smith

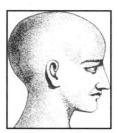

© 1992
THE CRITICAL THINKING CO.™
Phone: 800-458-4849 Fax: 831-393-3277
www.CriticalThinking.com
P.O. Box 1610 • Seaside • CA 93955-1610
ISBN 978-0-89455-441-4

ABOUT THE AUTHORS

George Bundy Smith is an Associate Judge of the New York State Court of Appeals, New York's highest court, and hears appeals from both civil and criminal cases. He has been a judge since 1975, the first eleven years as a trial judge, and is also an Adjunct Professor of Law at Fordham University School of Law in New York City. Judge Smith obtained his secondary education from Phillips Academy in Andover, Massachusetts. He holds an undergraduate degree (B.A.) from Yale College, a law degree (LL.B.) from Yale Law School, and a Master of Arts and doctorate in Political Science from New York University. He has authored articles in law journals, contributed to several legal treatises, and written numerous legal decisions.

Alene L. Smith is an Associate Professor at Hunter College of the City University of New York. Dr. Smith holds a doctorate in education from Columbia University Teachers College. She has been at Hunter College in the Department of Curriculum and Teaching since 1985, where she teaches reading/language arts, children's literature, and social studies to undergraduate and graduate students. Dr. Smith has presented workshops at city, state, and national conferences and has done consulting in the area of literature/reading. Multicultural literature is one of her areas of expertise. She is the author of several articles about education and literature.

for

George, Jr. and Beth

The authors wish to express their gratitude for the help of Ms. Barbara Andrews in the preparation of this work.

CONTENTS

INTRODUCTION

YOU DECIDE! is designed to help students develop an objective understanding of the rights and laws which have evolved, and continue to evolve, from the Bill of Rights. The book provides enriching opportunities for the students to

- examine and discuss actual Supreme Court cases, both as students giving their own opinions and as judges who must try to apply the principles of law without prejudice;

- explore how the amendments are applied in the legal system today;

- discover the history of these rights and learn about the Founding Fathers' struggle to insure that these rights became a part of the U.S. Constitution;

- develop a greater appreciation of the importance and the influence of the Bill of Rights in their daily lives.

Students will find the often contrasting viewpoints between their personal beliefs and their rulings as judges to be enlightening, thought-provoking experiences. They will learn that deciding cases in a judicial role requires that they resist snap decisions, ignore their personal feelings and prejudices, and evaluate cases according to the facts of the case, the rights granted by specific Amendments, and the interpretation of these rights according to judicial precedents set in other cases.

USING THE STUDENT TEXT AND THE TEACHER'S MANUAL

The student text and teacher's manual are meant to be used together as an enriching supplement to the regular curriculum. Student texts may be used as consumable items or one book can be reproduced for single-classroom use. The Teacher's Manual is not reproducible except for the blackline master of the Guide for Analyzing Cases on page 137.

The Student Text

The first lesson in each chapter of the student text uses one or two cases to introduce a general discussion. The cases involve the rights associated with the amendment or amendments that will be studied in the chapter. This gives students an opportunity to express their opinions prior to learning about an amendment. It also allows the teacher to assess the knowledge that students may have about the amendment. In addition, students will be able to use their responses in this lesson as a comparison/contrast to similar questions and issues later in the chapter.

The lessons that follow in each chapter lead students through activities designed to give them a comprehensive knowledge of each amendment. These lessons provide

- an examination of the language of each amendment and an opportunity for students to put this language into their own terms;

- a chance to analyze and discuss some past decisions of the Supreme Court;

- a brief study of the history of each amendment;

- a review of how judges today apply the laws related to the Bill of Rights;

- various activities that encourage students to apply their new knowledge of the Bill of Rights as judges who must review and decide real Supreme Court cases.

Working in cooperative small groups and total class discussions will keep students involved at all times in their own learning process. Sharing ideas and processing information together as they analyze, debate, and discuss issues will help increase students' comprehension of the materials. It will also help them recognize the strengths and weaknesses in their own reasoning and problem-solving processes.

The Teacher's Manual

The Teacher's Manual provides a plan for each lesson. These lesson plans give the teacher guidelines for

- the amount of time to allow for a lesson;

- preparing materials (for teachers who choose to reproduce the student text);

- lesson objectives for the students;

- a statement to motivate students at the beginning of the lesson;
- procedural development of the lesson;
- student homework assignments;
- teacher preparation for the next day's lesson;
- answers.

These lesson plans are simply suggestions for how the book might be used. The teacher is invited to use the lesson plans as presented, to modify them, to alter them to accommodate the knowledge, abilities, and special needs of the students, or to develop his/her own.

The answers provided in this manual are generally taken from the student text. In some cases, additional background or commentary is also provided. Teachers may find this additional information useful for keeping students focused on the issues. Where a question calls for student's opinions, often no answer is provided, although in some instances guidelines are given so that the teacher can aid students in their discussions.

SPECIAL NOTES FOR THE TEACHER

Racial Terms and Identification — Some of the cases deal with sensitive issues and a few terms have been kept in the actual historical context of court decisions. For example, the word "Negro" is used in one court decision. It was the accepted term for persons of African descent at the time the court decision was handed down and is therefore part of the historical picture. The term has not been changed for this text. A very few cases give the race of the defendants, victims, or law enforcement officers because race was an important element in how the cases were handled and decided. These cases played a significant role in the Supreme Court's definition of many of the civil rights granted to all the people under the Bill of Rights.

Language Comprehension — Many words and phrases used in the amendments are not commonly used in the same way now as they were when the amendments were written. For example, a phrase in the Sixth Amendment reads, "the accused shall *enjoy* the right to a speedy and public trial." This does not mean that the accused will have a good time at the trial, but rather that the accused will have the benefit of a speedy and public trial. The study of these changes in language provides an opportunity for vocabulary enrichment and for linkage between the social studies and language arts.

Students' abilities to interpret correct word meanings and phraseology of the amendments and to project the scope of intent by the writers of the Constitution and Bill of Rights is important to their ability to understand and evaluate court decisions. Clarifying terms can provide for lively class discussions as well as a vocabulary check.

The teacher will need to monitor students' understanding of legal terms used in the text. Some terms are commonly misinterpreted, such as *assault* and *battery*; others are confused as synonymous, such as *slander* and *libel*; while a few, such as *felony* and *misdemeanor*, need to be differentiated by degree.

Guide for Analyzing Cases — The teacher will need to make multiple copies of the Guide for Analyzing Cases from the blackline master on page 137 so that a good supply is on hand for students to use as needed. An alternative technique would be to provide students with one copy to use as a model in drawing additional Guides for themselves.

Dates of Cases — Sometimes the year in which a case was decided might clarify an otherwise confusing ruling by the Supreme Court. For example, a case may have been decided one way before the *Miranda* case and another way afterward. Be certain that students pay attention to the dates listed for cases.

Students' Case Notebooks — Beginning with the first lesson, students will be asked to develop a notebook of articles relevant to the Bill of Rights from newspapers and magazines and to take notes from news reports on television and radio. This notebook will provide students with a collection of current legal cases and issues to analyze and share with the class.

How and when items from students' notebooks are best used is up to the discretion of the teacher. In Chapters One and Two of the teacher's manual, however, a few suggestions for use are provided in the Development sections.

If possible, have students keep these articles and notes in a loose-leaf notebook. This will allow students to organize these materials according to the amendments involved. Notebooks should also include teacher handouts of material, student's completed Guides for Analyzing Cases, and the notes from their homework. This will help them to access information more easily when they need "evidence" to prove a point.

Using Graphic Organizers — To help students manage the facts and information in *You Decide!* it can be very helpful to supply, or to have students develop, a variety of graphic organizers.[1] With these organizers students can, among other tasks

- take notes on news items;

- set up and organize evidence for arguments or debates about issues;

- list assenting and dissenting court opinions;

- compare and contrast modern and historical word meanings;

- chart the history of the key persons, events, and documents that led to the adoption of the Bill of Rights.

Additional Reading and Research — If additional information about a case is needed or desired, any law school library, bar association, and most public libraries carry the United States Supreme Court cases in volumes of the *United States Reports*.

CRITICAL THINKING QUESTIONS FOR USE IN GROUP DISCUSSIONS

- Let's examine why you feel so strongly about this issue? How does it affect you personally?

- Let's see if we are letting our own personal opinions interfere with our making a fair decision. Let's examine the consequences of the decision.

- Before we continue, let's review what we have learned so far about this issue.

- Why do you think that is a good answer?

- Where did you find that information?

- What valid points do you see for the opposition?

- Do you think it's a good idea to be able to amend the Constitution? Why or why not?

- Does anyone else have a different answer or idea about this issue?

- Compare this situation with the other one. How are they the same or different?

- What circumstances make this a different kind of case from the other one?

- Why do you think this decision works in this case and not in the other?

- Based on this new information, how would you evaluate the judge's decision now?

- Why do you think this law is still applicable?

- Do you perceive weaknesses in this decision?

- How do you feel about the dissenting opinion?

- What are the weak and strong points in the argument?

- How should a judge determine which amendment right should receive the most attention in a case?

- Based on what you observe happening in society today, what would you change or add to this decision?

- Does anyone have an example of this from the newspaper or other news media?

- What are some advantages to everyone having the same opinion or "sentiment" about an issue?

- What are some advantages to people having diverse opinions and ideas about an issue?

- What possible negative or positive effects could this court decision have on you personally? on someone you know? on the majority of people? on a minority group?

- Since they had the same information, why and how did the judge(s) on the lower court reach a different decision from that of the judge(s) on the higher court?

---

1. *Organizing Thinking*, Books I and II, are supplemental books of reproducible graphic organizers designed to integrate higher order thinking skills across the curriculum. Available from Critical Thinking Press & Software, P.O. Box 448, Pacific Grove, CA 94950, (800) 458-4849.

CHAPTER ONE: THE FIRST AMENDMENT

LESSON ONE: YOU BE THE JUDGE

Teacher Preparation

READ / REVIEW
1. Student book — the Introduction, the Bill of Rights, the Guide for Analyzing Cases, Lesson One, and the Activity for Lesson One.
2. Teacher's manual — the Introduction and the Suggested Answers to the Activity for Lesson One.

MATERIALS
Student book — make copies of the Introduction, the Guide for Analyzing Cases, the Bill of Rights, Lesson One, and the Activity for Lesson One.

Also make copies of Lesson Two (What Does the First Amendment Say?) and the Activity for Lesson Two to distribute at the end of class.

If desired, make an overhead transparency of the Guide for Analyzing Cases and the Bill of Rights to review with the whole class.

Classroom Procedure

TIME
1–2 class periods

OBJECTIVES
The students will be able to:
1. Identify the amendments to the Constitution which make up the Bill of Rights.
2. Identify some of the rights granted by the Bill of Rights.
3. Utilize a Guide for Analyzing Cases.
4. Make judgments about cases cited.

MOTIVATION
Tell the students, "In this book we are going to be examining each of the amendments that make up the Bill of Rights. We are also going to learn to pull relevant information from real law cases and analyze how these cases relate to the Bill of Rights."

DEVELOPMENT
1. Engage the students in a general discussion to see what they already know about the Bill of Rights. Begin by asking them, "How many amendments make up the Bill of Rights?"

2. Ask if they are familiar with any of the amendments and how they have heard about the amendments. Ask if they know how the Bill of Rights came to be.

3. Tell the students, "We are going to begin by looking at two cases related to the First Amendment."

4. Distribute the materials for this lesson and allow students time to read through them.

5. Tell the students, "There is a way to organize and analyze the information in each case that you will be studying in this book. It is the sheet titled 'Guide for Analyzing Cases' which you received in your packet of materials. We are going to fill out the first Guide together as a class using the first case you read in Lesson One, *Wisconsin v. Yoder*."

6. Have the students take out their copy of the Guide for Analyzing Cases and also look at *Wisconsin v. Yoder*. Ask them question 1 in the Guide: "What are the main facts of the case." As students provide main facts, write each one on an overhead or on the board. Use the completed sample on the following page to help guide students' answers.

7. Work at filling out the rest of the Guide in this way. Students should be able to deduce the answer to question 2. When you get to questions 6 and 7, tell students, "In some cases, the Supreme Court decision is not given so that you will have an opportunity to judge a case for yourself. If a decision is not given, write 'information not given' for these questions."

8. Now read questions 1 and 2 of the Activity for Lesson One and ask for student responses.

9. Divide the students into small groups and let them discuss Case 2, *Edwards v. South Carolina*. Have each group fill out a Guide for Analyzing Cases. The students should appoint one of their group to record their answers on the Guide.

10. When the groups have filled out their Guides, they should also answer questions 3 and 4 in the Activity for Lesson One.

11. When the students have completed their work, have them come back together as one large group to discuss their responses. After students have given their opinions, review and discuss the actual Supreme Court decisions in each case (see the Suggested Answers, Activity for Lesson One).

12. Tell the students that they should begin collecting and organizing articles from newspapers and periodicals about cases or incidents that relate to the amendments which make up the Bill of Rights. These articles can serve as resources for discussion throughout the book. Students may also wish to take notes about cases or incidents they see on television or

hear about on the radio. (See the introduction to this manual
for additional suggestions.)

13. Distribute and discuss the assignment for Lesson Two.

**STUDENT
ASSIGNMENT
FOR THE NEXT
LESSON**

Have the students read Lesson Two (What Does the First
Amendment Say?) and do the Activity for Lesson Two.

Suggested Answers

**ACTIVITY FOR
LESSON ONE**

Case 1: *Wisconsin v. Yoder*, 406 U.S. 205 (1972) –
Guide for Analyzing Cases

(A completed sample of the Guide for Analyzing Cases is
shown below to serve as a model. After this, answers to the
Guide for all other cases will appear in regular text form.)

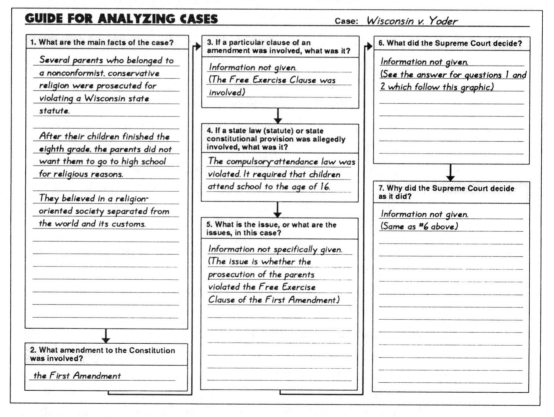

GUIDE FOR ANALYZING CASES   Case: *Wisconsin v. Yoder*

1. What are the main facts of the case?

Several parents who belonged to a nonconformist, conservative religion were prosecuted for violating a Wisconsin state statute.

After their children finished the eighth grade, the parents did not want them to go to high school for religious reasons.

They believed in a religion-oriented society separated from the world and its customs.

2. What amendment to the Constitution was involved?

the First Amendment

3. If a particular clause of an amendment was involved, what was it?

Information not given.
(The Free Exercise Clause was involved)

4. If a state law (statute) or state constitutional provision was allegedly involved, what was it?

The compulsory-attendance law was violated. It required that children attend school to the age of 16.

5. What is the issue, or what are the issues, in this case?

Information not specifically given.
(The issue is whether the prosecution of the parents violated the Free Exercise Clause of the First Amendment)

6. What did the Supreme Court decide?

Information not given.
(See the answer for questions 1 and 2 which follow this graphic)

7. Why did the Supreme Court decide as it did?

Information not given.
(Same as #6 above)

Answers to Questions 1 and 2 – *Wisconsin v. Yoder*:

The Wisconsin statute clearly said that children had to attend
school until age 16. Thus the parents' conduct would be a violation of that statute unless there was a more important reason
for allowing the students to leave school after the eighth grade.

The Supreme Court found that the Free Exercise Clause of the First Amendment was a good reason not to enforce the Wisconsin statute among the Amish. It should be noted, however, that the education of the Amish youth did not end when they left the public school in the eighth grade. They were continually trained to become useful citizens in the Amish community.

Case 2: *Edwards v. South Carolina*, 372 U.S. 229 (1963) – Guide for Analyzing Cases

1. The main facts of *Edwards v. South Carolina* are:
   a. Black high school and college students marched to the State House in Columbia, South Carolina.
   b. The students wanted to protest racial segregation and discrimination in South Carolina.
   c. They walked through the grounds carrying placards.
   d. About 200 to 300 onlookers watched.
   e. The students were told to leave within 15 minutes.
   f. The students were arrested when they did not leave and were prosecuted for breach of the peace.
2. The First Amendment was involved.
3. Information not given. (The clauses granting freedom of speech, freedom to peaceably assemble and to petition the government for a redress of grievances were involved.)
4. A statute was involved which made it unlawful to breach the peace.
5. Information not given. (The issue or problem was whether the police action violated the First Amendment rights of the students. Put another way, did the students have a right to protest in the way that they did?)
6. Information not given. (See the answers for questions 3 and 4 below.)
7. Information not given. (Same as #6 above.)

Answers to Questions 3 and 4 – *Edwards v. South Carolina*:

The students clearly were doing nothing to breach the peace. Their demonstration was a peaceful one. It is true that the demonstration may have aroused some anger in the onlookers. If so, the students were entitled to the protection of the police.

The Supreme Court decided that the arrest of the students was a clear violation of the First Amendment. It decided that the students were acting in a way that was guaranteed by the First Amendment. The peaceful assembly and march around the State House with placards was a classic way to protest and to seek a redress of grievances.

LESSON TWO: WHAT DOES THE FIRST AMENDMENT SAY?

Teacher Preparation

READ / REVIEW   1. Student book — Lesson Two and the Activity for Lesson Two.

2. Teacher's manual — the Suggested Answers to the Activity for Lesson Two.

MATERIALS   Student book — make copies of Lesson Three (Some Past Decisions of the Supreme Court) and the Activity for Lesson Three to distribute at the end of class.

Classroom Procedure

TIME   1 class period

OBJECTIVES   The students will be able to:

1. State what the words of the First Amendment mean.
2. Explain what rights the First Amendment grants.

MOTIVATION   Tell the students, "Today we are going to identify the rights granted by the First Amendment."

DEVELOPMENT   1. Go over the Activity for Lesson Two, giving several students the opportunity to read the choices they made as alternatives to the words or phrases in the First Amendment. Ask them to tell why they made these choices. Any difference of opinion is acceptable as long as students can support their choices.

2. Ask one student to read his/her interpretation of what the First Amendment means. Then ask if there are any students who have significantly different interpretations. If so, ask them to give their interpretations and support their reasoning.

3. Ask the students to identify all the rights granted by the First Amendment. List their responses on the board or on the overhead, making certain they address the following six key points:

   – no established religion
   – free exercise of religion

- freedom of speech
- freedom of the press
- the right of the people to peaceably assemble
- the right of the people to petition the government for a redress of grievances

4. Distribute and discuss the assignment for Lesson Three.
5. Remind students to watch for and collect media articles about First Amendment issues.

STUDENT ASSIGNMENT FOR THE NEXT LESSON

Have the students read Lesson Three (Some Past Decisions of the Supreme Court) and do the Activity for Lesson Three. Provide students with enough Guides so that they have one for each case.

Suggested Answers

ACTIVITY FOR LESSON TWO

Below are the most appropriate choices from the three alternatives provided. Be prepared to accept students' other choices as long as they are able to support their answers.

1. pass
2. concerning
3. adoption by the state
4. forbidding
5. practice
6. limiting
7. liberty to speak one's mind
8. news media
9. power
10. gather together
11. urge
12. correction
13. wrongs

LESSON THREE: SOME PAST DECISIONS OF THE SUPREME COURT

Teacher Preparation

READ / REVIEW
1. Student book — Lesson Three and the Activity for Lesson Three.
2. Teacher's manual — the Suggested Answers to the Activity for Lesson Three.

MATERIALS
Student book — make copies of Lesson Four (What Are the Origins of the Religion Clauses of the First Amendment?) and the Activity for Lesson Four to distribute at the end of class.

Classroom Procedure

TIME
1–2 class periods

OBJECTIVES
The students will be able to:
1. Identify some of the key issues in First Amendment cases.
2. Apply knowledge gained about the First Amendment to cases that are cited.
3. Make judgments about cases.

MOTIVATION
Tell the students, "Today we are going to analyze some First Amendment cases. Let's review the six key ideas in the First Amendment.

Congress shall make no law:

– respecting an establishment of religion;

– prohibiting the free exercise of religion;

– abridging the freedom of speech;

– abridging the freedom of the press;

– abridging the right of the people to peaceably assemble;

– abridging the right of the people to petition the government for a redress of grievances."

DEVELOPMENT
1. Divide the students into four groups and assign each group one of the cases in Lesson Three. Distribute a blank Guide to each group and have them select one person from the group to fill out their Guide.

2. Have the students discuss the cases they have been assigned, using the completed Guides from their homework to aid their discussions.

3. Each group should identify the key issues in their case by comparing the answers in their Guides. Where there is disagreement, have the students discuss the issue and try to reach a common decision. The recorder in each group should fill out a Guide, with the answers agreed upon by the group, to present to the class. Also, each group should be prepared to answer the questions: "Do you agree or disagree with the decision of the Court in the case you were assigned? Why or why not? How would you decide the case?"

4. When the students have completed the assignment, have them reassemble as a total class. Have one member of each group present its case, including whether or not they agree with the decision of the Court, their reasons, and how they would decide the case.

5. After a group has presented its findings, open the discussion to the rest of the class.

6. Use the board or overhead to record highlights of each case.

7. Distribute and discuss the assignment for Lesson Four.

STUDENT ASSIGNMENT FOR THE NEXT LESSON

1. Have the students read Lesson Four (What Are the Origins of the Religion Clauses of the First Amendment?). Tell them to use the Activity for Lesson Four to help guide their reading.

2. Students should be prepared to answer and discuss the questions in the Activity for Lesson Four. Have them make an outline noting the key information in their reading to help them in their discussions.

Suggested Answers

ACTIVITY FOR LESSON THREE

Case 1: *Everson v. Board of Education of The Township of Ewing*, 330 U.S. 1 (1947) – **Guide for Analyzing Cases**

This is one of a number of cases in which the Supreme Court of the United States and other courts have struggled to determine what the Establishment Clause of the First Amendment means and what aid, if any, can be given to religious and sectarian schools.

1. The main facts of the case are:

   a. A state statute and a local rule authorized reimbursement to parents for money spent in transporting their children to school.

    b. Some reimbursement went to parents whose children attended Catholic parochial schools.

    c. The Catholic schools taught both secular education and religious education.

    d. A taxpayer sued to prevent reimbursement to parents who sent their children to parochial schools.

    e. The taxpayer stated that the reimbursement violated the First Amendment.

2. The First Amendment was involved.

3. The case involved the Establishment Clause.

4. The statute permitted reimbursement to parents whose children attended Catholic schools.

5. The issue or problem was whether the reimbursement violated the Establishment Clause of the First Amendment.

6. The Supreme Court decided that reimbursement to the parents was permissible and did not violate the First Amendment.

7. Information not given. (The Supreme Court said that this reimbursement was not aiding religion. It was assisting a valid state policy of seeing that children traveled safely to and from school.)

Case 2: *Torcaso v. Watkins,* 367 U.S. 488 (1961) – Guide for Analyzing Cases

This case upholds the Constitution and the First Amendment by permitting the freedom to exercise or not to exercise a religion. It should be noted that Article VI of the Constitution requires senators and representatives, members of the state legislatures, and all executive and judicial officers of the United States and the several states to support the Constitution by oath or affirmation. The same Article states, however, that "no religious Test shall ever be required as a Qualification to any Office or public Trust under the United States."

1. The main facts of the case are:

    a. The Governor of Maryland appointed a person to the position of Notary Public.

    b. The person, in order to serve, had to declare a belief in God according to the constitution of the state of Maryland.

    c. The appointee refused to declare a belief in God.

2. The First Amendment was involved.

3. The Free Exercise (of religion) Clause was involved.

4. A provision of the Maryland State Constitution was violated. It required that appointees declare their belief in God.

5. The issue was whether the requirement that an appointee declare a belief in God violated the Free Exercise Clause of the First Amendment.

6. The Supreme Court ruled that the provision of the Maryland Constitution was unconstitutional.

7. Information not given. (The Supreme Court stated that the provision of the Maryland Constitution was a violation of a person's right to exercise religion or not to exercise it as the person saw fit. There could be no religious test or requirement to hold a public office.)

Case 3: *Chaplinsky v. New Hampshire,* 315 U.S. 568 (1942) – Guide for Analyzing Cases

This is one of a number of cases in which the Supreme Court has dealt with speech which may be unacceptable to the majority of a community. In *Chaplinsky* the court discussed a speaker's right to speak and any limitations on that right.

1. The main facts in *Chaplinsky* are as follows:
   a. The defendant, Chaplinsky, belonged to a religious sect known as Jehovah's Witnesses and was distributing its literature on the streets.
   b. While distributing the literature, the defendant called all religion a "racket." People were annoyed at his comments and a crowd near him became agitated.
   c. A traffic officer led Chaplinsky to a police station. They met the city marshal on the way and Chaplinsky and the marshal became involved in an argument.
   d. Chaplinsky made uncomplimentary remarks about the marshal and the government in Rochester.
   e. He was arrested and convicted for using offensive language in public.
   f. His conviction was affirmed by the Supreme Court of New Hampshire. Chaplinsky then appealed to the U.S. Supreme Court.

2. The case involved the First Amendment.

3. The Freedom of Speech clause was involved.

4. The law allegedly violated was a New Hampshire statute which made it illegal to use "offensive, derisive, or annoying" words in public or to call another person an "offensive or derisive" name.

5. The issue was whether the arrest or conviction of the defendant violated the right to freedom of speech.

6. The Supreme Court ruled that the conviction did not violate the First Amendment and should be affirmed.

7. The Supreme Court stated that the words used tended to incite a breach of the peace and were not protected by the First Amendment.

Case 4: *Near v. Minnesota*, 283 U.S. 697 (1931) – Guide for Analyzing Cases

This is a classic case in which the Supreme Court upheld the right of newspapers and other publications to print without government restraint or censorship.

1. The main facts in *Near* are as follows:

    a. In 1927 in Minneapolis, Minnesota, a series of articles were printed in a publication called the *Saturday Press*.

    b. The articles stated that a Jewish gangster was in charge of gambling, racketeering, and other criminal activities in Minneapolis and that many criminals there were Jewish.

    c. The articles also said that many public officials, including the Mayor, were not doing their jobs.

    d. A Minnesota statute allowed the District Court in Minneapolis to grant an order against publication. The District Court issued such an order.

    e. The Supreme Court of Minnesota affirmed the order. The case then went to the U.S. Supreme Court.

2. The First Amendment was involved.

3. The Freedom of Speech and of the Press Clauses were involved.

4. A Minnesota law permitted a county attorney or other public official to bring a lawsuit to prevent the publication of a newspaper that printed malicious, scandalous, and defamatory material.

5. The issue was whether the Minnesota statute violated the freedom of speech and of the press by placing a prior restraint on publication.

6. The Supreme Court determined that the Minnesota statute was unconstitutional because it violated the freedom of speech and of the press guaranteed by the First Amendment.

7. The Supreme Court ruled that the Minnesota statute was an impermissible prior restraint on publication. In other words, it was a violation of the First Amendment to prevent publication of a newspaper. It also stated that if the newspaper's accusations were false, a person could sue the newspaper for damages after publication.

LESSON FOUR: WHAT ARE THE ORIGINS OF THE RELIGION CLAUSES OF THE FIRST AMENDMENT?

Teacher Preparation

READ / REVIEW   1. Student book — Lesson Four and the Activity for Lesson Four.

2. Teacher's manual — the Suggested Answers to the Activity for Lesson Four.

MATERIALS   Student book — make copies of Lesson Five (The First Amendment Today–Religion) and Activities 1 and 2 for Lesson Five to distribute at the end of class. (Lesson Five has seven activities which can be done over three to four class periods. See the note at the beginning of Lesson Five, Part I, in this manual for an overview of the assignments.)

Classroom Procedure

TIME   1 class period

OBJECTIVES   The students will be able to:

Identify the three major factors leading to the sentiment for a constitutional amendment protecting religious freedom and become familiar with some of the people and events that played major roles in this process.

MOTIVATION   Tell the students, "Today's discussion will focus on the origins of the religion clauses of the First Amendment."

DEVELOPMENT   1. Tell the students, "There were three important factors which led to increased sentiment for religious freedom. Let's look at Lesson Four and discuss what these factors were." (Discuss the meaning of *sentiment* as used here if any students are having difficulty understanding this term.)

2. Read each question in the activity and allow the students to share the answers from their homework assignment. Make certain that students support their reasoning.

3. Use the board or overhead to highlight the students' key points for each question.

4. Distribute and discuss the assignment for Lesson Five, Part I.

STUDENT ASSIGNMENT FOR THE NEXT LESSON

Have the students read Lesson Five, A–C, and do Activities 1 and 2 for Lesson Five. (They will read Lesson Five D in a later assignment.)

Suggested Answers

ACTIVITY FOR LESSON FOUR

Questions 1–6

1. An established religion in America meant that the government supported a particular religion or denomination or supported more than one religion or denomination. Often support was financial, that is, money given by the government for the salaries of clergymen and for church buildings.

   Arguments in favor of established religion might include:

   a. A society free of conflict because the beliefs and practices of all people would be the same.

   b. The absence of conflict between religions which in history have sometimes been extremely bitter.

   The strongest argument against an established religion is that it forces people to pretend to believe and/or practice things which are contrary to their real views.

2. Group feelings for or against a condition.

3. Roger Williams was banished from the Massachusetts Bay Colony in 1635 because he believed that the church and state should be kept separate and apart, and because he believed that the Puritans should not force others to conform to their beliefs. When he went to Rhode Island, Williams established a policy of tolerating all religions.

   William Penn and the Quakers in Pennsylvania had a policy of tolerating all religions.

   James Madison wrote a paper called *Memorial and Remonstrance Against Religious Assessments* in 1784. It was written at a time when the Virginia legislature was debating a bill on whether or not to extend an assessment, or tax, to support religion. Madison argued that religion and the state should be separate and that different religions should be tolerated.

4. This document argued for the separation of church and state and for religious toleration.

5. This statute permitted the free exercise of religion in Virginia. It was one of the major events leading to the sentiment for freedom of religion that eventually resulted in an amendment in the Bill of Rights.

6. Any answer is acceptable as long as a student can support his/her reasoning.

LESSON FIVE, PART I: THE FIRST AMENDMENT TODAY – RELIGION

NOTE   Lesson Five is divided into three parts in the Teacher's Manual—I, II, and III. Part I uses Activities 1 and 2 for Lesson Five, Part II uses Activities 3, 4, and 5 for Lesson Five, and Part III uses Activities 6 and 7 for Lesson Five. Completion of these activities may take up to four class periods.

Teacher Preparation

READ / REVIEW
1. Student book — Lesson Five, sections A–C, and Activities 1 and 2 for Lesson Five.
2. Teacher's manual — the Suggested Answers to Activities 1 and 2 for Lesson Five.

MATERIALS
Student book — make copies of Activities 3, 4, and 5 for Lesson Five to distribute at the end of the class.

Classroom Procedure

TIME
1 class period

OBJECTIVES
The students will be able to:
1. Explain the significance of the Due Process Clause of the Fourteenth Amendment and indicate its relationship to the First Amendment.
2. Define *an establishment of religion* according to both Justice Hugo Black and Justice William Rehnquist.
3. Recall the three tests used in the *Lemon v. Kurtzman* case to determine if a statute violates the Establishment Clause.

MOTIVATION
Ask the students, "How many have heard the expression 'deprive any person of life, liberty, or property, without due process of law'? What do you think it means? We will discuss the meaning of this expression in today's lesson."

DEVELOPMENT
1. Discuss Activities 1 and 2 for Lesson Five as a class. Make certain students are able to support the reasoning for their answers.
2. Discuss particularly the significance of the Due Process Clause. Help the students see the relationship between the Fourteenth Amendment and the First Amendment.

3. As students identify the three tests used in *Lemon v. Kurtzman* to determine whether the Establishment Clause has been violated, note these on the board or overhead.

4. Distribute and discuss the assignment for Lesson Five, Part II.

STUDENT ASSIGNMENT FOR THE NEXT LESSON

1. Have the students review all of Lesson Five C (What Does *An Establishment of Religion* Mean?) and do Activities 3, 4, and 5 for Lesson Five.

2. Half of the students should be prepared to debate the question "What does an establishment of religion mean?" using Justice Black's opinion; the other half should be prepared to debate the same question using Justice Rehnquist's opinion.

3. The students should make an outline or use their answers from Activity 2, questions 4 and 5, to help them prepare for the debate.

Suggested Answers

ACTIVITY 1 FOR LESSON FIVE

Comprehension Quick Check

1. Yes
2. No
3. No

ACTIVITY 2 FOR LESSON FIVE

Questions 1–6

1. *Barron v. Mayor and City Council of Baltimore* (32 U.S. [7 Pet.] 242) was an 1833 case in which the Supreme Court stated that the Bill of Rights was a limitation on the federal government but not on the state governments. (This meant, for example, that while the federal government could not abridge the freedom of speech or of the press, the states were under no such restraint under the federal Bill of Rights.) The opinion that the Bill of Rights applied only to the federal government prevailed until *Gitlow v. New York* (268 U.S. 652) in 1925. In *Gitlow*, the Supreme Court ruled that the First Amendment placed limits on state and local governments as well as on the federal government. Today almost all of the amendments in the Bill of Rights apply to the state governments.

2. The Fourteenth Amendment was added to the Constitution in 1868 after the Civil War. One of its primary purposes was to make freed slaves citizens of the United States. The Fourteenth Amendment contains what is known as a Due Process

Clause. It reads that no state "shall deprive any person of life, liberty, or property, without due process of law." The Supreme Court has held that the rights guaranteed by the First Amendment are part of the due process of law. The First Amendment is applicable to the states through the Due Process Clause of the Fourteenth Amendment.

3. The term means that religion and government should be kept separate and apart.

4. Justice Hugo Black served on the Supreme Court from 1937 to 1971. In *Everson v. Board of Education of the Township of Ewing*, Justice Black, writing for the majority, discussed the meaning of the term "establishment of religion." It meant that a wall of separation between church and state was required. Some of the things which he believed the state and federal governments could not do are quoted in the student text and below.

> The "establishment of religion" clause of the First Amendment means at least this: Neither a state nor the Federal Government can set up a church. Neither can pass laws which aid one religion, aid all religions, or prefer one religion over another. Neither can force nor influence a person to go to or to remain away from church against his will or force him to profess a belief or disbelief in any religion. No person can be punished for entertaining or professing religious beliefs or disbeliefs, for church attendance or non-attendance. No tax in any amount, large or small, can be levied to support any religious activities or institutions, whatever they may be called, or whatever form they may adopt to teach or practice religion. Neither a state nor the Federal Government can, openly or secretly, participate in the affairs of any religious organizations or groups and vice versa. In the words of Jefferson, the clause against establishment of religion by law was intended to erect "a wall of separation between Church and State." (*Reynolds v. United States*, supra [98 U.S. at 164, 25 L.ed 249]).

From this quotation it is clear that Black believed neither the state nor the federal government could do the following:

a. Set up a church.
b. Pass laws to aid one religion or all religions.
c. Pass laws to prefer one religion over another.
d. Force or influence a person to go to church against his/her will.

   e. Force or influence a person to remain away from church against his/her will.

   f. Force a person to believe a religion.

   g. Force a person to disbelieve a religion.

   h. Punish a person for professing religious beliefs.

   i. Punish a person for not professing religious beliefs.

   j. Levy a tax to support religious activities.

   k. Participate in the affairs of a religious organization or group either openly or in secret.

5. Justice Rehnquist was appointed to the Supreme Court in 1972 and became Chief Justice in 1986. In a dissent in *Wallace v. Jaffree* (472 U.S. 38 [1985]), Justice Rehnquist disagreed that the Establishment Clause meant a wall of separation between church and state. To him it meant only that the government could not establish a national religion and could not prefer one religion over another.

   Justice Rehnquist also said that the Founding Fathers did not advocate a wall of separation between church and state. He also believed that the *Lemon* three-prong test for determining if a particular statute violated the First Amendment was difficult to apply. As for a law having a secular purpose, a legislature could always say there was a secular purpose. On the other hand, one purpose of any legislation to aid students in religious schools was to aid the school itself. Thus, no aid to religious schools, including bus transportation for pupils, was permissible under this secular purpose test. The third requirement in *Lemon*, no excessive entanglement by government in religion, itself required the government to become excessively involved in religious schools in order to insure that this requirement was met.

6. *Lemon v. Kurtzman* (403 U.S. 602 [1971]) is a case in which the Supreme Court attempted to establish the following three tests for determining whether a statute breached the wall of separation of church and state.

   a. A statute must have a secular not religious purpose.

   b. The principal effect of the statute should not be to aid or inhibit religion.

   c. A statute should not foster excessive entanglement with religion.

LESSON FIVE, PART II: THE FIRST AMENDMENT TODAY – RELIGION (cont.)

Teacher Preparation

READ / REVIEW
1. Student book — review Lesson Five C; read Activities 3, 4, and 5 for Lesson Five.
2. Teacher's manual — the Suggested Answers to Activities 3, 4, and 5 for Lesson Five.

MATERIALS
Student book — make copies of Activities 6 and 7 to distribute at the end of class.

Classroom Procedure

TIME
2 class periods

OBJECTIVES
The students will be able to:
1. Debate either Justice Black's or Justice Rehnquist's position regarding the Establishment Clause.
2. Determine whether the cases in Activity 4 show violations of the Establishment Clause according to Justice Black's decision in *Everson* and the three tests used in *Lemon v. Kurtzman*.
3. Determine whether the cases in Activity 4 show violations of the Establishment Clause according to Justice Rehnquist's dissenting opinion in *Wallace v. Jaffree*.

MOTIVATION
Tell the students, "Two outstanding Supreme Court justices have different opinions about what the Establishment Clause means. Today we are going to debate their opinions."

DEVELOPMENT
1. Divide the students into two groups. One group will debate Justice Black's view, the other group, Justice Rehnquist's.
2. Give each side time to meet together to go over their ideas.
3. Ask the two groups, "What do you think an establishment of religion means according to the First Amendment?"
4. Each side should then be given enough time to state their views.

5. Highlight, or have a student highlight, the groups' views on the board or overhead.

6. After students have had an opportunity to debate their views, help the students sum up both sides of the issue.

7. The students should discuss their answers to Activities 4 and 5 as a class and give reasons for their answers.

8. Distribute and discuss the assignment for Lesson Five, Part III.

STUDENT ASSIGNMENT FOR THE NEXT LESSON

1. Have the students review Lesson Five, C and read Lesson Five D (What Does the Free Exercise of Religion Mean?).

2. Have the students do Activities 6 and 7 for Lesson Five.

===

Suggested Answers

ACTIVITY 3 FOR LESSON FIVE

Student Debate – Justice Black's and Justice Rehnquist's opinions regarding the Establishment Clause

As an alternative to the debate, have a class discussion of the points in both Justice Black's and Justice Rehnquist's opinions.

ACTIVITY 4 FOR LESSON FIVE

Cases 1–4

Case 1: *Everson v. Board of Education of the Township of Ewing,* 330 U.S. 1 (1947)

The students should give their own views.

Justice Black wrote *Everson* and stated that reimbursing the parents for transportation did not violate the Establishment Clause. Reimbursement would also appear not to violate *Lemon v. Kurtzman.* The secular purpose is bus transportation.

In its ruling, the Supreme Court permitted parents of parochial school children to receive reimbursement for transportation expenses. Reimbursement for transportation to school is not an aid or hindrance to religion. There is no excessive entanglement of government and religion. Also, the state had an interest in seeing that children were transported safely to school.

Case 2: *Engel v. Vitale,* 370 U.S. 421 (1962)

The students should state their own views.

The fact that a state legislature or government body requires a prayer to be said in school seems to violate the "wall of separation" required by *Everson.*

The requirement of a prayer violates the first test in *Lemon*—that the statute have a secular, not religious, purpose. The requirement also violates the second test in that it aids religion.

The Supreme Court held the prayer violated the Establishment Clause of the First Amendment. A governmental body could not compose a prayer and direct that it be used in schools.

Case 3: *Witters v. Washington Department of Services for the Blind,* 474 U.S. 481 (1986)

The students should state their opinions.

This statute, when applied to a person who is attending a religious school, is, arguably, a violation of the *Everson* case. The aid for attendance at a religious school seems to violate the "wall of separation" doctrine.

The statute does not seem to violate the tests used in *Lemon*. First, the statute has a secular, not religious, purpose. It is to aid visually handicapped students in general, not just those attending a divinity school. Second, the primary effect of the statute is not to aid or inhibit religion. Third, the statute does not require excessive or even any entanglement with religion or religious doctrine.

In this case the Supreme Court held that a statute which authorized aid to the visually handicapped (the young man was gradually losing his eyesight) did not violate the Establishment Clause. The young man wished to attend a private Christian College to become a pastor, missionary, or youth director. The court noted that aid was provided to the visually handicapped in general, not just to those who wanted to attend religious schools. The court also noted that the aid went to the recipient and not directly to the institution.

Case 4: *School District of the City of Grand Rapids v. Ball,* 473 U.S. 373 (1985)

The students should state their opinions.

The fact that programs in sectarian schools were being funded by government seemed to breach the "wall of separation" doctrine in *Everson*.

The statute, arguably, could be said to violate or not violate the *Lemon* test. On the one hand, it could be argued that the assistance was for programs which were completely secular (math, reading, Spanish). From this point of view, the statute has a secular purpose, it does not aid or hinder religion and it does not involve an excessive entanglement with religion.

On the other hand, looked at from another viewpoint, the statute reasonably could be said to violate *Lemon*. A primary purpose of the statute was to assist sectarian schools. Second, a principal effect of the statute might be to send a message of state support for religion. Another effect was to relieve sectarian schools of the necessity of providing some secular courses while being free to teach religion.

The Supreme Court ruled that the Grand Rapids program violated the Establishment Clause for three reasons. First, the teachers might be influenced by the sectarian nature of the environment and subtly or overtly influence the students' religious beliefs. Second, because of the state involvement, a message of state support for religion was given. Third, the programs subsidized some religious functions in the schools by taking over and providing for secular education.

ACTIVITY 5 FOR LESSON FIVE This activity calls for the students to review the four cases in Activity 4 for Lesson Five and to compare them to Justice Rehnquist's view of the meaning of the Establishment Clause. If his test is used, there would be no violation of the Establishment Clause. Specifically, none of the cases requires the establishment of a national religion. Moreover, none of the cases requires the preference of one religious sect or denomination over the other.

LESSON FIVE, PART III: THE FIRST AMENDMENT TODAY – RELIGION (cont.)

Teacher Preparation

READ / REVIEW
1. Student book — review Lesson Five C; read Lesson Five D, and Activities 6 and 7 for Lesson Five.
2. Teacher's manual — the Suggested Answers for Activities 6 and 7 for Lesson Five.

MATERIALS
Student book — make copies of Lesson Six and Activities 1 and 2 for Lesson Six to distribute at the end of class.

Classroom Procedure

TIME
1 class period

OBJECTIVES
The students will be able to:
1. Choose which opinion (Black's or Rehnquist's) they feel serves as the best test of whether or not the establishment clause has been violated.
2. Define what the free exercise of religion means.
3. State their opinions regarding cases related to the Free Exercise Clause.

MOTIVATION
Tell the students, "Today we are going to review the opinions of Justice Black and Justice Rehnquist regarding the Establishment Clause. Then we are going to look at the issue of the Free Exercise Clause of the First Amendment."

DEVELOPMENT
1. Engage the students in Activity 6 for Lesson Five. Have them restate the opinions of Justices Black and Rehnquist and express which opinion they think serves as the best test of whether or not the Establishment Clause has been violated.
2. Have the students give definitions of what the Free Exercise Clause means. They should be able to do this from their homework assignments. Ask the students, "How do you think the Supreme Court determines if this clause is being violated?"
3. Engage the students in Activity 7 for Lesson Five. Have them look at three cases: Lesson 1, Case 1: *Wisconsin v. Yoder,*

Lesson 3, Case 2: *Torcaso v. Watkins*, and the case provided in Activity 7, *McDaniel v. Paty* (435 U.S. 618 [1978]).

3. Allow the students to discuss the cases and give their opinions. Do they feel the cases show a violation of the Free Exercise Clause? The students should give reasons for their answers.

4. Distribute and discuss the assignment for Lesson Six.

STUDENT ASSIGNMENT FOR THE NEXT LESSON

Have the students read Lesson Six (What Are the Origins of the Freedom of Expression Clauses In the First Amendment?) and do Activities 1 and 2 for Lesson Six.

Suggested Answers

ACTIVITY 6 FOR LESSON FIVE

Discuss students' decisions as a total class. Ask students to give reasons for their decisions.

Comment on Activity 6 for Lesson Five: This activity seeks to have the students indicate their preference for the Black view of the Establishment Clause (as expressed in *Everson-Lemon*) or the Rehnquist view (in the dissent of *Wallace v. Jaffree*). It also seeks the students' reasons for choosing as they do. It should be understood that the question does not ask the students to come to a conclusion about what the Founding Fathers intended by the Establishment Clause. This question is purely one of opinion. It seems clear that if the Black view is preferred, there will be little assistance of any kind to sectarian (religious) schools. If the Rehnquist view is preferred, there will be such assistance.

ACTIVITY 7 FOR LESSON FIVE

Cases 1–3

Case 1: *Wisconsin v. Yoder*

In this case the Supreme Court held that the Wisconsin statute requiring youngsters to attend school until age 16 violated the Free Exercise Clause of the First Amendment.

On the one hand, a student can argue that the requirement to attend school until age 16 is reasonable and even necessary to prepare a person for life. Thus there would be no violation of the Free Exercise Clause because the requirement is a reasonable one.

On the other hand, a student can argue that the requirement of school attendance to age 16 violates the Free Exercise Clause because it forces the Amish community to give up its way of life and interferes with that community's efforts to educate and prepare its youngsters for life in that community.

Case 2: *Torcaso v. Watkins*

In this case the Supreme Court ruled that the state of Maryland could not require a person to take an oath in order to hold a public office.

The requirement of a religious oath is a clear violation of the Free Exercise Clause of the First Amendment. That clause permits any person to choose a religion or not to choose it.

Case 3: *McDaniel v. Paty*, 435 U.S. 618 (1978)

In this case the Supreme Court held that a religious leader could not be barred from serving as a delegate to a constitutional convention. A majority of the justices believed that there was a violation of the Free Exercise Clause.

The prohibition against service in a constitutional convention would seem to be a clear violation of the right to freely exercise one's religion.

LESSON SIX: WHAT ARE THE ORIGINS OF THE FREEDOM OF EXPRESSION CLAUSES IN THE FIRST AMENDMENT?

Teacher Preparation

READ / REVIEW 1. Student book — Lesson Six and Activities 1 and 2 for Lesson Six.

2. Teacher's manual — the Suggested Answers to Activities 1 and 2 for Lesson Six.

MATERIALS Student book — make copies of Lesson Seven and Activity 1 for Lesson Seven to distribute at the end of class. (Lesson Seven has two activities which can be done over three class periods. See the note at the beginning of Lesson Seven, Part I, in this manual for an overview of the assignments.)

Classroom Procedure

TIME 1 class period

OBJECTIVES The students will be able to:

1. Recall the historical events that influenced the writing of the First Amendment Freedom of Expression Clauses.

2. Explain the roles of John Lilburne, John Peter Zenger, and William Blackstone in relation to the First Amendment.

3. Identify the major steps in placing the First Amendment into the Constitution.

MOTIVATION Tell the students, "Today we are going to discuss freedom of expression and the people and events which led to the adoption of the Freedom of Expression Clauses in the First Amendment."

DEVELOPMENT 1. Use the Activities for Lesson Six to engage the students in a discussion about the origins of the First Amendment Freedom of Expression Clauses.

2. Have the students recall the historical events that influenced the writing of these clauses. Discuss the struggles for free expression in England and in the American colonies.

3. Have the students explain the roles of John Lilburne, John Peter Zenger, and William Blackstone.

4. Have the students list the major steps in placing the First Amendment into the Constitution. Write these steps on the board or overhead.

5. Distribute and discuss the assignment for Lesson Seven, Part I.

STUDENT ASSIGNMENT FOR THE NEXT LESSON

1. Have the students read Lesson Seven (The First Amendment Today – Freedom of Expression), A–B3.

2. The students should be prepared to discuss questions 1–3 in Activity 1 for Lesson Seven.

Suggested Answers

ACTIVITY 1 FOR LESSON SIX

Questions 1–4

1. The Licensing Act of 1662, passed by the English Parliament, allowed the government to control criticism against it in three ways: 1) it allowed royal officials to investigate and seize printed works which criticized the government; 2) it stipulated that all works published in England had to be licensed beforehand; 3) it made it possible to imprison anyone who published works critical of the government.

    These methods were also used by the English in the American colonies to repress critical works there. Colonists' reaction against these methods created a strong feeling that freedom of expression was a basic right which should be protected. This sentiment lead to the Freedom of Expression Clauses in the First Amendment.

2. John Lilburne was an Englishman charged with printing seditious books. He was imprisoned for many years but eventually had his sentence lifted as illegal and was given money to make amends. His case represents the continuing struggle in England and America to establish the rights of citizens to freely express their thoughts—even if that expression is critical of the government.

3. John Peter Zenger was a German immigrant to America who was accused of and tried for printing works which attacked the government of England. The jury in his case found him not guilty because, it stated, the truth was a defense.

    The jury's decision in this case set a precedent for defending freedom of expression. This precedent reinforced the colonists' firm belief that freedom of the press and freedom of expression were rights which the government could not take away. They later protected these freedoms by including them in the First Amendment.

4. William Blackstone was an English jurist who wrote *Commentaries on the Laws of England* (1765–69). In these commentaries he advocated the position that there could not be an order preventing a work from being published. Blackstone's position that there could be no prior restraint on publication was an important influence on the writers of the First Amendment.

ACTIVITY 2 FOR LESSON SIX

The major steps in placing the First Amendment into the Constitution were:

— Some of the delegates to the state constitutional conventions called for a bill of rights.
— Some (delegates to conventions in Maryland, Massachusetts, New Hampshire, South Carolina, New York, North Carolina, Pennsylvania, and Virginia) urged various amendments to the proposed constitution. Some of these amendments became a part of the Bill of Rights.
— James Madison, "Father of the Constitution" and a U.S. Congressman from Virginia, announced that he favored amendments.
— In Congress, on June 8, 1789, Madison proposed several amendments to the Constitution, one of which was to become the First Amendment.
— On August 24 and September 9, 1789, respectively, the House of Representatives and the Senate approved some of the amendments.
— On September 25, 1789, the Congress of the United States approved a Bill of Rights containing the First Amendment.
— The final step was to forward the First Amendment and other amendments to the states for ratification.
— On December 15, 1791, the Bill of Rights went into effect when Virginia became the thirteenth state to ratify their addition to the Constitution.

LESSON SEVEN, PART I: THE FIRST AMENDMENT TODAY–FREEDOM OF EXPRESSION

NOTE Lesson Seven is divided into two parts in the Teacher's Manual—I and II. Part I uses Activity 1, questions 1–3 for Lesson Seven; Part II uses Activity 1, questions 4–7, and Activity 2 for Lesson Seven. Completion of these activities may take three class periods.

Teacher Preparation

READ / REVIEW
1. Student book — Lesson Seven A (Application of the Free Expression Clauses of the First Amendment) through B3 (Symbolic Speech). Also read Activity 1 for Lesson Seven, questions 1–3.

2. Teacher's manual — the Suggested Answers to questions 1–3 for Activity 1 for Lesson Seven.

MATERIALS
Student book — make copies of Activity 2 for Lesson Seven to distribute at the end of class.

Classroom Procedure

TIME
1 class period

OBJECTIVES
The students will be able to:
1. Infer the opposite point of view from Justice Hugo Black's notion of an absolute guarantee of freedom of speech.
2. Decide why the Supreme Court made the decision it did in *Edwards v. South Carolina*.
3. Explain the meaning of three of the Free Expression Clauses of the First Amendment.
4. Explain the meaning of symbolic speech.

MOTIVATION
Tell the students, "Historically, the First Amendment applied only to the federal government. What allowed the First Amendment to be applied to the states? Can you recall the case that changed this application and what clause is involved?"

DEVELOPMENT
1. Have the students go over questions 1–3 of Activity 1 for Lesson Seven.
2. Discuss Justice Hugo Black's definition of freedom of speech.
3. Have the students infer what the opposite point of view from Justice Black's might be.

4. Have the students explain why they believe the Supreme Court made the decision it did in *Edwards v. South Carolina*. Ask them whether they agree with the decision and to give reasons why they do or do not.

5. Have the students explain the meaning of three of the Free Expression Clauses: free speech, free assembly, and the right to petition for redress of grievances.

6. Have the students define symbolic speech and give examples.

7. Distribute and discuss the assignment for Lesson Seven, Part II.

STUDENT ASSIGNMENT FOR THE NEXT LESSON

1. Have the students read Lesson Seven, B4–D.
2. Have them answer questions 4–8 of Activity 1, read the cases in Activity 2 for Lesson Seven, and answer the questions following each case.

Suggested Answers

ACTIVITY 1 FOR LESSON SEVEN

Questions 1–3

1. By an absolute guarantee of freedom of speech, Justice Black meant that the government could not pass a law prohibiting freedom of speech under almost any circumstances.

2. The Supreme Court reversed the convictions of the college students because it determined that the prosecutions and convictions of the students violated their rights to free speech, free assembly, and the freedom to petition the government for redress of grievances.

    (Let several students state whether or not they agree with the decision of the Court. Be certain they support their reasoning based on what they have learned about the First Amendment.)

3. Symbolic speech is conduct or action by people that communicates an idea. It may or may not be accompanied by words. As a type of speech, symbolic speech can seek protection under the First Amendment.

    (Let the students offer their opinions about what might be considered symbolic speech. They should use examples not found in their lesson. Examples might include: wearing of arm bands, sitting while everyone stands, standing while everyone sits, raising a clenched fist.)

LESSON SEVEN, PART II: THE FIRST AMENDMENT TODAY – FREEDOM OF EXPRESSION (cont.)

Teacher Preparation

READ / REVIEW
1. Student book—Lesson Seven, B4–D, Activity 1 for Lesson Seven, questions 4–8, and Activity 2 for Lesson Seven.

2. Teacher's manual—the Suggested Answers to Activity 1 for Lesson Seven, questions 4–8, and for Activity 2 for Lesson Seven.

MATERIALS
Student book—make copies of Lesson Eight and Activities 1 and 2 for Lesson Eight to distribute at the end of class.

Classroom Procedure

TIME
1–2 class periods

OBJECTIVES
The student will be able to:
1. Identify three areas where limits are placed on free speech.

2. Explain the terms: *clear and present danger, fighting words, freedom of association,* and *prior restraint.*

3. Compare and contrast cases related to the Free Expression Clauses of the First Amendment and make judgments about those cases.

MOTIVATION
Tell students, "Often we think of free speech as having no limits. Today we will discuss three areas in which speech can be constitutionally limited."

DEVELOPMENT
1. Go over the homework assignment, Activity 1 for Lesson Seven, questions 4–8.

2. Include in the discussion the three areas where limits are placed on free speech.

3. Allow time for the students to explain, in their own words: *clear and present danger, fighting words, freedom of association,* and *prior restraint.*

4. Activity 2 for Lesson Seven could be used as part of today's activities and/or used on a second day. The students should

compare and contrast the cases presented and make judgments about them. Use the questions following each case to help guide students in their discussions.

5. Distribute and discuss the assignment for Lesson Eight.

STUDENT ASSIGNMENT FOR THE NEXT LESSON

1. Have the students review Lessons Four–Seven.
2. Have them read Lesson Eight and Activities 1 and 2 for Lesson Eight. They should be prepared to discuss Activities 1 and 2 for the next class.
3. Have the students bring to class their clippings or media notes regarding First Amendment issues or cases to help them in their discussions.

Suggested Answers

ACTIVITY 1 FOR LESSON SEVEN

Questions 4–8

4. Three areas of free speech in which some limits do apply are national security, fighting words, and obscenity.

5. The "clear and present danger" test is a guideline which a judge can apply to a case to determine whether someone's speech presents a threat to national security. The clear and present danger test was originally formulated in *Schenck v. United States* (249 U.S. 47 [1919]). At the time it appeared to prohibit any speech that advocated the overthrow of the government by force and violence. In various decisions between *Schenck* in 1919 and *Brandenburg v. Ohio* (395 U.S. 444) in 1969, the Court discussed the clear and present danger test. The meaning of clear and present danger depended on the facts and the views of the judges writing about the doctrine.

    In the *Brandenburg* decision, the Supreme Court articulated as a group what some judges had argued for some time—namely that there was a difference between mere advocacy (stating that a particular action should be taken) and incitement (urging that immediate action be taken).

    In sum, the clear and present danger test has changed from a doctrine which looks merely at the words spoken without concentrating on the effect those words might have on conduct or action to one which looks at words in terms of what their effect will be on immediate action.

6. Fighting words are words that can be expected to provoke a hostile reaction in a reasonable person.

7. Freedom of association means that people have a right to

band together to express similar views or band together to participate in a common form of worship.

8. Prior restraint is preventing publication of a newspaper, periodical, or other printed material.

ACTIVITY 2 FOR LESSON SEVEN

Comparing Some First Amendment Cases

Case 1: *Feiner v. People of the State of New York,* **340 U.S. 315 (1951)**

The Supreme Court of the United States discussed *Feiner v. New York* in its decision in *Edwards v. South Carolina.* It stated that the cases were different. It noted that the protesters in *Edwards* were quiet and peaceful and that the onlookers were not unruly. It should be noted, however, that the line between proper assertion of First Amendment rights by protesters has not always been easy to determine. It is also true that a government could place reasonable limits on where, when, and how to exercise First Amendment rights. For example, traffic problems or regulations are relevant on the issue of protest marches.

In answering the questions, a student might take the view, as did Justice Hugo Black, that Feiner was exercising his freedom of speech and that the police should have protected that right. If this view is taken, there was a violation of Feiner's rights when he was arrested. On the other hand, a student can argue that there are limits to free speech and that Feiner exceeded the bounds of free speech with his remarks. If this view is taken, there was no violation of his First Amendment rights.

The Supreme Court upheld Feiner's conviction. It stated that Feiner's speech had passed "the bounds of argument or persuasion" and become an "incitement to riot."

Case 2: *Elrod v. Burns,* **427 U.S. 347 (1976)**

In this case, the Supreme Court ruled that the new sheriff of Cook County, Illinois, could not dismiss persons in nonpolicy-making jobs simply because they were not of his political party. Five of the nine justices could not agree on a single opinion. Three justices of the five-member majority felt that to dismiss the employees was a violation of their right to their own political beliefs and associations. Two others in the majority stated that the jobs were non-policy-making and there was no showing of inadequate performance by the employees.

A strong argument can be made that to fire people from non-policy-making positions where there is no showing of inadequate performance is a violation of the right to hold one's own political beliefs and to associate with those of similar views. If this argument is accepted, a judge should require the sheriff of Cook

County to keep the old employees. The First Amendment and its guarantee of the right to freedom of association would be violated by the firing.

Case 3: *Nebraska Press Association v. Stuart,* 427 U.S. 539 (1976)

In this case the Supreme Court held that a ban on publication of a confession or statement of the accused and a ban on reporting what happened at a preliminary hearing was a violation of the freedom of the press.

A prior restraint on publication is impermissible. As to whether the order was necessary to protect the accused's right to a fair trial, as a general rule (with limited exceptions), court proceedings must be open to the public. In order to exclude the press from the criminal proceedings, the person accused, or the prosecution, would have to make a strong argument showing that the defendant's rights would be prejudiced if the confession were published or if a report of the court proceedings where the confession was discussed were made public.

The case of *Nebraska Press Association v. Stuart* presents an example of the conflict between First Amendment rights and the rights of a person accused of crime.

LESSON EIGHT: JUDGE FOR YOURSELF

Teacher Preparation

READ / REVIEW
1. Student book — Lesson Eight and Activities 1 and 2 for Lesson Eight.
2. Teacher's manual — the Suggested Answers to Activities 1 and 2 for Lesson Eight.

MATERIALS
No materials are needed for homework. The first lesson of Chapter Two (The Fourth Amendment) will be done as an in-class activity.

Classroom Procedure

TIME
2 class periods

OBJECTIVES
The students will be able to:
1. Give their opinions about the purposes of First Amendment guarantees today.
2. Act as judges and make decisions about cases that deal with the First Amendment.
3. Apply the knowledge they have learned to analyze articles and cases related to the First Amendment that have been collected outside of the classroom.

MOTIVATION
Tell the students, "Today we are going to use the knowledge we have gained about the First Amendment to analyze and make judgments about some cases."

DEVELOPMENT
1. Have several students share their answers to Activity 1 for Lesson Eight. Discuss students' answers as a check on their comprehension of Lessons Four through Seven.
2. Using the Guide for Analyzing Cases, lead a discussion of each case in Activity 2 for Lesson Eight. Ask students for their responses to both the Guide and to the questions following each case.
3. Give students additional opportunities to apply the knowledge they have gained by having them discuss cases and issues from their collection of articles and media notes. If it

would be helpful, use the Guide for Analyzing Cases to help students in their discussions.

STUDENT ASSIGNMENT FOR THE NEXT LESSON

The next lesson is an in-class assignment.

Suggested Answers

ACTIVITY 1 FOR LESSON EIGHT

Questions 1–10

1. Yes
2. Yes
3. Yes
4. No
5. No
6. Yes
7. No
8. Yes
9. Yes
10. Yes

ACTIVITY 2 FOR LESSON EIGHT

Cases 1–6

Case 1: *Board of Trustees of the Village of Scarsdale v. McCreay*, 471 U.S. 83 (1985)

1. The main facts of the case are:
   a. A creche (a display of the scene at the birth of Jesus Christ) was permitted in a public park during the Christmas season for several years.
   b. The creche was paid for by a group of churches, and a sign was displayed that indicated the creche was not sponsored by the local government.
   c. In both 1981 and 1982 permission to display the creche was denied by the Board of Trustees of Scarsdale.
   d. Some residents sued to obtain permission to display the creche.
   e. A federal district court ruled that the display violated the Establishment Clause.
   f. The federal appeals court then ruled the display did not violate the Establishment Clause.
   g. The case was appealed to the Supreme Court.
2. The First Amendment was involved.

3. The case involved the Establishment Clause.

4. No state law or state constitutional provision was allegedly violated.

5. The issue was whether the display of a creche, a religious display, in a public park violated the Establishment Clause of the First Amendment.

6. Information not given. (The Supreme Court was divided 4-4 [One of the nine justices did not participate]. Therefore, the decision of the Court of Appeals for the Second Circuit was affirmed. The Second Circuit ruled that the creche could be displayed in the park.)

7. Information not given. (The Second Circuit used the three-prong *Lemon* test to determine if there was a violation of the Establishment Clause. Among its reasons for finding no violation, the Second Circuit said that the use of the park had no direct and immediate effect in advancing religion, the government did not bear the expense, and a sign indicated that the government did not sponsor the creche.)

Answers to Questions 1 and 2 following Case 1:

The 4-4 tie vote in the Supreme Court demonstrates the difficulty in arriving at a decision on whether the Establishment Clause was violated. The display was religious and for this reason an argument could be made that the government was supporting religion by allowing the display in a public park. On the other hand, the fact that the government did not pay for the display, disclaimed any responsibility for it, and simply gave access to a public park for the display supports the position of those who say that the three-prong *Lemon* test was not violated.

Case 2: *Employment Division, Department of Human Resources of Oregon v. Alfred L. Smith*, 494 U.S. 872, 110 S. Ct. 1595 (1990)

1. The main facts in this case are:
    a. Two individuals were fired from their jobs at a private drug rehabilitation facility in Oregon because they used an illegal hallucinogenic drug, peyote, in connection with religious practices in their Native American Church.
    b. The two sought unemployment benefits which were denied because they had been fired for misconduct.
    c. They appealed this decision first to the Oregon Court of Appeals then to the Oregon Supreme Court. Both courts ruled that withholding their benefits denied the two persons their right to the free exercise of their religion.

d. The case then went to the U.S. Supreme Court.

2. The First Amendment was involved.

3. The case involved the Free Exercise Clause.

4. The State of Oregon had a law which made it illegal to possess peyote. Oregon also had a law which said that an employee who was fired for misconduct could not obtain unemployment benefits.

5. The issue was whether the Free Exercise Clause of the First Amendment protected the use of the illegal drug peyote so that the men were entitled to receive unemployment benefits.

6. Information not given. (The Supreme Court upheld the denial of benefits.)

7. Information not given. (The Supreme Court concluded that illegal drugs could not be used even as a religious practice. There was no violation of the Establishment Clause. Unemployment benefits were properly denied.)

Answers to Questions 1–3 following Case 2:

A judge must have a basis for ruling as he or she does. In this case, a judge could grant the unemployment benefits only if s/he concluded that the use of peyote as a religious practice was permissible and that any prohibition against its use violated the First Amendment's Free Exercise Clause. It must be emphasized, however, that all religious practices are not protected by the First Amendment. Thus the use of illegal drugs would not be permitted even as a part of religious practices.

As specific answers to the three questions: 1) the judge should deny the benefits; 2) there is no violation of the Free Exercise Clause if there is a denial; 3) the Free Exercise Clause does not permit illegal practices as a part of religion.

Case 3: *Bethel School District No. 403 v. Fraser*, 478 U.S. 675 (1986)

1. The main facts of the case were:
   a. A high school student gave a speech at an assembly and nominated another student for elective office.
   b. The student used sexually explicit language.
   c. Some students were as young as 14 years of age.
   d. Prior to the assembly the student was warned that the language was inappropriate.
   e. The day after his speech the student was told that he was suspended for three days and could not be a graduation speaker.

    f. The student, by his father as guardian *ad litem*, sued the school district.

    g. The student believed that the punishment violated his right to freedom of speech.

2. The First Amendment was involved.

3. The case involved the Free Speech Clause.

4. No state law or state constitutional provision was allegedly violated. There was a school rule, however, which prohibited the use of obscene language or gestures.

5. The issue was whether the speech was protected by the First Amendment's guarantee of freedom of speech.

6. Information not given. (A federal district court said the punishment violated the First Amendment. Thus the student should be allowed to speak at graduation. An appeals court upheld the decision of the district court. By the time the case got to the Supreme Court, the student had graduated [and had been allowed to speak at his graduation]. However, because of its importance and because a similar issue could come up in the future, the Supreme Court decided the case. It ruled that the school authorities had the right to discipline the student as they did.)

7. Information not given. (The Supreme Court reversed the decision of the lower court because it held that the school authorities were within their rights in punishing speech which was "lewd" and "indecent.")

Answers to Questions 1 and 2 following Case 3:

The question of how to rule depends on the judge and his/her view of the First Amendment. It does seem, however, that the age of the audience would be relevant. Things might be said in an assembly of college students that would be inappropriate for younger people.

Case 4: *Texas v. Johnson,* 491 U.S. 397 (1989)

1. The main facts of the case are as follows:

    a. During the 1984 Republican National convention in Dallas, Texas, a political demonstration was held to protest the policies of President Ronald Reagan.

    b. During the demonstration, a young man named Johnson poured kerosene on the American flag and burned it.

    c. Johnson was arrested and convicted of desecrating the flag.

    d. The Texas Court of Criminal Appeals held that Johnson's arrest and prosecution violated his right to free speech.

    f. The case then went to the U.S. Supreme Court.

2. The First Amendment was involved.

3. The clause guaranteeing freedom of speech was involved.

4. A Texas statute made it illegal to desecrate or treat the flag with contempt.

5. The issue was whether Johnson's act of burning the flag was protected by the First Amendment.

6. Information not given. (The Supreme Court decided that Johnson should not have been convicted.)

7. Information not given. (The Supreme Court concluded that the demonstrator's conduct was expressive [symbolic speech] and protected by the First Amendment. The Texas statute was unconstitutional.)

Answers to Questions 1–3 following Case 4:

The vote in the Supreme Court was 5-4, and it is clear that the decision was controversial. Students could, arguably, decide the case either way, that is, to uphold the conviction or to reverse it. There is an argument that the act was symbolic speech protected by the First Amendment. In that case, the conviction would have to be reversed.

On the other hand, the dissent in *Johnson*, among other things, concluded that the act of burning the flag was conduct rather than speech and because of the importance of the flag, conduct which desecrated the flag could be regulated. If this view is taken, the burning of the flag is not symbolic speech protected by the First Amendment and the conviction could be upheld.

Case 5: *Branzburg v. Hayes*, 408 U.S. 665 (1972)

1. The main facts of the case are:

    a. On November 15, 1969, a reporter in Louisville, Kentucky, wrote a story for the *Courier Journal* newspaper about two persons illegally making hashish from marijuana.

    b. The reporter was ordered to appear before a grand jury which asked him to identify the persons who were making the hashish.

    c. The reporter appeared but refused to reveal the information on the grounds that it would violate freedom of the press.

    d. A state court ordered the reporter to answer the Grand Jury's questions. The reporter appealed but his appeal was refused.

    e. He then asked the Supreme Court to review his conviction.

2. The First Amendment was involved.

3. The case involved the Freedom of the Press Clause.

4. A state law made possession of marijuana illegal.

5. The issue was whether the order to appear and testify before a grand jury violated the right to freedom of the press.

6. Information not given. (The Supreme Court ruled that the reporter could be forced to appear and testify.)

7. Information not given. (The Supreme Court ruled that the freedom of the press would not prevent the reporter from appearing and testifying before a grand jury [Note: A number of states have passed "Shield Laws" which protect a reporter from revealing his or her sources].)

Answers to Questions 1 and 2 following Case 5:

Unless a state has passed a Shield Law to protect a reporter from revealing his/her sources, s/he can be required to appear before a grand jury and answer questions. Some people believe that such a requirement places an unwarranted limit on freedom of the press. It is felt that informants will not talk to reporters if they know the reporter can be forced to reveal the source of information. Thus a valuable source of information to the public will be cut off. If this view is taken, a reporter should not be required to appear before a grand jury and reporters should be protected from revealing their sources.

On the other hand, there are persons who argue that reporters, like anyone else, should be required to appear before a grand jury to give information on illegal activities. If this view is taken, there is no violation of the First Amendment and reporters should be required to reveal their sources.

Case 6: *Oklahoma Publishing Co. v. District Court in and for Oklahoma County, Oklahoma*, 430 U.S. 308 (1977)

1. The main facts of the case were:
   a. On June 26, 1976, a railroad worker was shot and killed in Oklahoma County, Oklahoma.
   b. An eleven-year old boy was charged with the killing.
   c. A court hearing was held at which reporters were present. After the hearing a photographer took a picture of the boy.
   d. The boy's name and picture were published in a newspaper.
   e. A court order was issued enjoining (prohibiting) the news media from further printing the picture or name of the boy.

2. The First Amendment was involved.

3. The case involved the Freedom of the Press Clause.

4. An Oklahoma statute required that juvenile proceedings be private, unless a judge ordered otherwise, and that juvenile records could be opened only by court order and to persons having a legitimate interest in the records.

5. The issue was whether the order was a prior restraint on the press in violation of the freedom of the press guaranteed by the First Amendment.

6. No information given. (The Supreme Court reversed the order of the Oklahoma Supreme Court.)

7. No information given. (The Supreme Court ruled that the order enjoining the publication was a prior restraint in violation of the First and Fourteenth Amendments to the Constitution.)

Answers to Questions 1 and 2 following Case 6:

The order prohibiting publication was a clear prior restraint on publication and a clear violation of the right of freedom of the press.

CHAPTER TWO: THE FOURTH AMENDMENT
Lesson One: YOU BE THE JUDGE

Teacher Preparation

READ/REVIEW

1. Student book — Lesson One and the Activity for Lesson One.
2. Teacher's Manual — the Suggested Answers to the Activity for Lesson One.

MATERIALS

Student book — make copies of Lesson One and the Activity for Lesson One for this class period. Also make copies of Lesson Two (What Does the Fourth Amendment Say?) and the Activity for Lesson Two to distribute at the end of class.

Classroom Procedure

TIME

1 class period

OBJECTIVES

The students will be able to:

1. Analyze a case related to the Fourth Amendment and decide whether police followed proper procedure in the case.
2. Share their thinking in a group situation.

MOTIVATION

Tell the students, "Today we are going to examine a case involving the Fourth Amendment and try to determine whether any Fourth Amendment rights were violated in this case."

DEVELOPMENT

1. Begin the lesson by assessing what the students already know about the Fourth Amendment. Ask the students a series of questions to get them to express their knowledge. For example:
   a. Does anyone know what rights are guaranteed by the Fourth Amendment?
   b. Are you familiar with any cases that involve an issue related to the Fourth Amendment?
2. Tell the students that this class period they will read a legal case involving the Fourth Amendment.

3. Distribute and have the students read Lesson One, Case 1: *Terry v. Ohio.*

4. Divide the students into small groups. Give each group a Guide for Analyzing Cases. Let them discuss the case as a group using the Guide. Each group should appoint a recorder to fill in the Guide.

5. Have each group also answer questions 1 and 2 following the description of the case.

6. Come back together as a large group to discuss the answers.

7. Have the students keep their answers for future discussions. Also, remind the students to continue collecting articles and cases relating to the first eight amendments of the Bill of Rights—especially articles about the Fourth Amendment for this unit.

8. Distribute and discuss the assignment for Lesson Two.

STUDENT ASSIGNMENT FOR THE NEXT LESSON

Have the students read Lesson Two (What Does The Fourth Amendment Say?) and do the Activity for Lesson Two.

Suggested Answers

ACTIVITY FOR LESSON ONE

Case 1: *Terry v. Ohio*, 392 U.S. 1 (1968) — Guide for Analyzing Cases

1. The main facts of the case are:
   a. A police detective suspected three men of wanting to rob a store.
   b. The detective feared the men might have guns and frisked them.
   c. Guns were found on two of the men.
   d. No weapon was found on the third man.
   e. All three men were taken to a police station and the two men who had guns were arrested.

2. The Fourth Amendment was involved.

3. Information not given. (The clause allegedly violated prohibited unreasonable searches and seizures of a person.)

4. The law violated was one which prohibited people from carrying concealed weapons without a license.

5. Information not given. (There were two issues in this case. The first issue was whether the police had a right to stop a

 ©*1992* **CRITICAL THINKING PRESS & SOFTWARE** • *P.O. Box 448, Pacific Grove, CA 93950*

person on less than probable cause or reasonable cause that the person had committed, was committing, or was about to commit a crime. The second issue was whether or not the police had a right to frisk a person to see if s/he had a weapon.)

6. Information not given. (The Supreme Court ruled that the stop and frisk were proper. It declined to suppress the guns as evidence in the trial.)

7. Information not given. (The Supreme Court ruled that when a police officer stopped someone on reasonable suspicion of criminal activity and, at the same time, the officer had a reasonable fear for his/her own safety, the officer had a right to frisk the suspect for weapons.)

Answers to Questions 1 and 2 following *Terry v. Ohio*:

1. The three men were properly stopped on reasonable suspicion of criminal activity because the detective feared they wanted to rob a store.

2. The Supreme Court concluded that where an officer feared for his or her safety, he or she had the right to frisk that person.

Comment: At the time the Supreme Court decided *Terry v. Ohio* in 1968, several states had passed what were known as *stop and frisk* laws (see Chapter Two, Lesson Five A1, in the student book). When the stop and frisk laws were used to stop, frisk, and ultimately arrest a person, they were challenged as unconstitutional.

The case of *Terry v. Ohio* was the first *stop and frisk* case decided by the Supreme Court of the United States. There were two issues in *Terry v. Ohio*. The first issue was whether the police had a right to stop a person on less than probable cause, or reasonable suspicion, that the person had committed, was committing, or was about to commit a crime. The Supreme Court held (ruled) that a person could be stopped on reasonable suspicion of criminal activity or potential criminal activity.

The second issue in *Terry* was whether or not the police had a right to frisk (pat down) a person to see if he or she had a weapon. The Supreme Court held that a police officer had a right to protect himself; therefore, if the officer had a reasonable fear for his safety, the officer could frisk the person to see if he or she had a weapon.

LESSON TWO: WHAT DOES THE FOURTH AMENDMENT SAY?

Teacher Preparation

READ / REVIEW
1. Student book — Lesson Two and the Activity for Lesson Two.
2. Teacher's Manual — the Suggested Answers for Lesson Two. As background, also read Lesson Four (What Are the Origins of the Fourth Amendment?) and Lesson Five (The Fourth Amendment Today).

MATERIALS
Student book — make copies of Lesson Three (Some Past Decisions of the Supreme Court) and the Activity for Lesson Three to distribute at the end of class.

Classroom Procedure

TIME
1–2 class periods

OBJECTIVES
The students will be able to:
1. State what they believe the words of the Fourth Amendment mean.
2. Explain what rights the Fourth Amendment grants.

MOTIVATION
Tell the students, "Today we are going to examine and identify the meaning of the words of the Fourth Amendment"

DEVELOPMENT
1. Go over the activity for Lesson Two, giving several students an opportunity to read the choices they made as alternatives to the words or phrases in the Fourth Amendment. Ask them why they made these choices. Any choice is acceptable as long as the student can support his/her choice.
2. Ask one student to read his/her interpretation of what the Fourth Amendment means. Ask if other students have significantly different meanings and, if so, to support their reasoning.
3. Ask the students to identify (and note on the board or overhead) all the rights granted by the Fourth Amendment. Make certain they address the following key points:

       — no unreasonable searches and seizures of peoples' selves, houses, papers, and effects

       — no warrants issued except those supported by religious oath or personal promise of truthfulness

       — no warrants issued except those that are specific about the place to be searched, the person to be searched, or the thing to be searched for

4. Distribute and discuss the assignment for Lesson Three.

STUDENT ASSIGNMENT FOR THE NEXT LESSON

Have the students read Lesson Three (Some Past Decisions of the Supreme Court) and do the Activity for Lesson Three. Since there are five cases in the lesson, you may want to make this two assignments. Make certain that students have a Guide to fill out for each case.

Suggested Answers

ACTIVITY FOR LESSON TWO

Below are the most appropriate choices from the three alternatives provided. Be prepared to accept students' other choices as long as they are able to support their choices.

1. to have control over
2. bodies
3. belongings
4. arbitrary
5. forceful taking
6. abused
7. order of a judge to seize property or search for property
8. be made
9. strong evidence
10. promise to God to be truthful
11. promise to be truthful (nonreligious)
12. specifically
13. stating
14. examined
15. taken

LESSON THREE: SOME PAST DECISIONS OF THE SUPREME COURT

Teacher Preparation

READ / REVIEW   1. Student book — Lesson Three and the Activity for Lesson Three.

2. Teacher's manual — the Suggested Answers to the Activity for Lesson Three.

MATERIALS   Student book — make copies of Lesson Four (What Are the Origins of the Fourth Amendment?) and the Activity for Lesson Four to distribute at the end of class.

Classroom Procedure

TIME   1–2 class periods

OBJECTIVES   The students will be able to:

1. Identify some of the key issues in Fourth Amendment cases.

2. Apply knowledge gained about the Fourth Amendment to cases that are cited.

3. Indicate why they believe the Supreme Court decided as it did in various cases.

MOTIVATION   Begin the lesson by telling the students, "Today (and tomorrow) we are going to look at some cases that involve Fourth Amendment rights and the following issues:
– stopping and frisking a person
– searching a home
– eavesdropping on a telephone
– searching an automobile
– searching a person's discarded garbage."

DEVELOPMENT   1. Divide the students into five groups. Assign each group one of the five cases in Lesson Three. Distribute a blank Guide to each group and have each group select a recorder to fill out their Guide.

2. Have the students discuss the cases they have been assigned,

using the completed Guides from their homework to aid their discussions.

3. Each group should identify the key issues in their case by comparing the answers in their Guides. Where there is disagreement, have the students discuss the issue and try to reach a common decision. The recorder in each group should fill out a new Guide, with the agreed upon answers, which they can present to the class. Also, each group should be prepared to answer the questions: "Do you agree or disagree with the decision of the Court in your case? Why do you think the court ruled as it did? How would you decide the case?"

4. When the students have completed the assignment, have them reassemble as a total class. Have one member of each group present its case, including whether or not they agree with the decision of the Court, their reasons, and how they would decide the case.

5. After a group has presented its findings, open the discussion to the rest of the class.

6. Use the board or overhead to record highlights of each case.

7. Distribute and discuss the assignment for Lesson Four.

STUDENT ASSIGNMENT FOR THE NEXT LESSON

Have the students read Lesson Four (What Are the Origins of the Fourth Amendment?) and do the Activity for Lesson Four.

Suggested Answers

ACTIVITY FOR LESSON THREE

Cases 1–5

Case 1: Person–Stop and Frisk—*Sibron v. New York*, 392 U.S. 40 (1968) — Guide for Analyzing Cases

1. The main facts of the case are:
   a. A police officer saw a man speak to six or eight known drug addicts.
   b. Later the officer saw the man speak to three other known drug addicts.
   c. Both times the officer did not see the man hand anything to or take anything from the drug addicts.
   d. The police officer went up to the man and said, "You know what I am after."
   e. The officer put his hand into the man's pocket and pulled out several thin, translucent envelopes.

     f. The envelopes turned out to contain cocaine.

     g. The man was arrested for possession of cocaine.

2. The Amendment involved was the Fourth Amendment.

3. Information not given. (The clause allegedly violated prohibited unreasonable searches and seizures of a person.)

4. The law violated was a state law which prohibited the possession of cocaine.

5. The issue was whether the officer had the right to stop and search the man.

6. The Supreme Court ruled in favor of the defendant. (The court ruled that the drugs seized from Sibron had to be suppressed.)

7. The Supreme Court stated that the police had no right to search the defendant.

Comment: This case involved a stop and frisk statute. The Supreme Court decided that the defendant had done nothing except talk to people. (Since he had done nothing to suggest criminal activity, there was insufficient evidence for the officer to make a forcible stop in order to question him.) Moreover, there was no indication that the officer feared for his safety. Therefore, the Supreme Court ruled that the drugs seized from Sibron had to be suppressed and could not be used against him in a trial.

Case 2: Home—*Mapp v. Ohio*, 367 U.S. 643 (1961) — Guide for Analyzing Cases

1. The main facts of the case are:

     a. Police officers in Cleveland, Ohio, went to the home of a woman and told her that they were looking for a man whom they wanted to question about a recent bombing. They also said that they were looking for evidence of a policy or numbers operation.

     b. The officers waited outside while the woman called her lawyer; she then refused to allow the police to enter.

     c. The police had no search warrant.

     d. They broke in and searched the house where they found books and papers which they claimed were obscene.

     e. They arrested the woman for possession of obscene materials.

2. The Amendment involved was the Fourth Amendment.

3. Information not given. (The clause allegedly violated prohibited unreasonable searches and seizures of a person's house.)

4. The state law allegedly violated prohibited the possession of obscene materials.

5. The issues were: 1) whether the officers had the right to enter Mapp's home without a warrant, and 2) whether the evidence taken could be introduced in a state court.

6. The Supreme Court ruled that the officers had no right to enter the home and that the evidence taken could not be introduced in a state court.

7. The Supreme Court ruled this way because it wanted to stop improper police conduct. It had been the law since 1914 that illegally seized evidence was not admissible in federal courts.

Comment: *Mapp v. Ohio* was the first time that the Supreme Court ruled that improperly seized evidence could not be admitted in state courts. It had been the law since 1914 (*United States v. Weeks*, 232 U.S. 383) that improperly seized evidence was not admissible in federal courts. The main reason for excluding such evidence from the courts was to deter and stop improper police conduct. The Supreme Court found that there was no reasonable basis for excluding improperly seized evidence from federal courts while admitting such evidence in state courts. The Supreme Court concluded that a logical interpretation of the Constitution, specifically the Fourth and Fourteenth Amendments, required the exclusion of improperly seized evidence from both state and federal courts.

Case 3: Eavesdropping—*Katz v. United States*, 389 U.S. 347 (1967) — Guide for Analyzing Cases

1. The main facts of the case are:
   a. FBI agents suspected that a man was placing bets illegally over the telephone.
   b. A device was attached to a telephone booth so that the FBI could overhear his conversations.
   c. The man was arrested and prosecuted for illegally betting by phone.

2. The Amendment involved was the Fourth Amendment.

3. Information not given. (The clauses allegedly violated prohibited unreasonable searches and seizures of a person or a person's effects.)

4. The federal law which was allegedly violated prohibited transmitting gambling information by telephone.

5. The issue was whether the Fourth Amendment was violated when the police eavesdropped on a telephone conversation without a warrant to do so.

6. The Supreme Court ruled that the police had no right to eavesdrop on the man without an eavesdropping warrant

and, therefore, the evidence (conversations overhead) could not be used against him.

7. The Supreme Court ruled this way because the evidence against him had been improperly obtained.

Comment: This was a case in which the Supreme Court determined that an eavesdropping warrant, signed by a judge and authorizing eavesdropping (wiretapping is an example of eavesdropping), was necessary before any eavesdropping could be done by the police. If eavesdropping was done without an eavesdropping warrant, there was a violation of the Fourth Amendment. Thus the case determined that the Fourth Amendment was applicable to eavesdropping even though the words of the Fourth Amendment do not explicitly prohibit eavesdropping.

Case 4: Automobiles—*Carroll v. United States*, 267 U.S. 132 (1925) — Guide for Analyzing Cases

1. The main facts of the case are:
   a. Undercover police officers went to an apartment in Grand Rapids, Michigan to purchase liquor illegally.
   b. At the time, December 1921, it was illegal to sell liquor in the U.S.
   c. In the apartment, three men agreed to sell the officers the liquor, then the three left the apartment saying they would return shortly.
   d. They drove away in an Oldsmobile Roadster automobile.
   e. One of the men returned later and said they could not get the liquor that night but would bring it back the next day.
   f. For reasons unknown, the men did not return the next day.
   g. Several days later the same policemen, patrolling a road leading from Detroit to Grand Rapids, Michigan, saw two men in the Oldsmobile Roadster which the three men selling liquor had used several days earlier.
   h. The officers believed that the two men in the car were the same ones who had been in the apartment and that they were transporting liquor illegally.
   i. The officers stopped and searched the car without a search warrant.
   j. They found liquor and arrested the two men for transporting liquor illegally.

2. The Amendment involved is the Fourth Amendment.

3. Information not given. (The clauses allegedly violated prohibited unreasonable searches and seizures of a person's effects.)

4. A federal statute was involved which prohibited the possession and transportation of liquor with the intent to violate the Eighteenth Amendment to the Constitution.

5. The issues were: 1) whether the police had *probable cause* to believe a crime was being committed and 2) whether the police could search a car without a warrant.

6. The Supreme Court ruled that the search of the car was proper.

7. The Supreme Court stated that there was probable cause to believe that liquor was being transported illegally. The reasons there was probable cause included the facts that liquor was often transported illegally from Detroit to Grand Rapids, the men were known to transport liquor illegally, and the officers had a prior experience with the men in which an agreement to sell liquor illegally to the undercover officers had been made (even though the men did not return to complete the deal).

Comment: This case established the automobile exception to the warrant requirement of the Fourth Amendment (see Lesson Five A4 in this chapter). This means that a warrant is not necessary for the police to search an automobile so long as the police have probable cause to believe that contraband (a gun, drugs, etc.) is in the car.

Case 5: Outside of a Home—*California v. Greenwood*, 486 U.S. 35 (1988) — Guide for Analyzing Cases

1. The main facts of the case were:
   a. Police officers in Laguna Beach, California, received information that a person was dealing in drugs.
   b. One police officer asked a garbage collector to bring her the person's garbage which had been put out on the sidewalk.
   c. The police had no warrant to search the garbage.
   d. The police found items among the garbage which indicated drug use.
   e. Based on these facts, the police obtained a search warrant for the house.
   f. In the house they found cocaine and hashish.
   g. They arrested the occupant of the house.

2. The amendment involved was the Fourth Amendment.

3. Information not given. (The clause allegedly violated prohibited the unreasonable search and seizure of a person's effects.)

4. The federal law allegedly violated prohibited the possession of cocaine and hashish.

5. The issue was whether the police had the right to search discarded garbage without a warrant.

6. The Supreme Court ruled that there was nothing improper about the search of the garbage.

7. The Supreme Court ruled as it did because the garbage had been put out on the sidewalk.

Comment: In this case, the Supreme Court ruled that once garbage had been placed outside of the house in a public area, no privacy interest was involved, and the garbage could be searched without a warrant.

LESSON FOUR: WHAT ARE THE ORIGINS OF THE FOURTH AMENDMENT?

Teacher Preparation

READ / REVIEW

1. Student book — Lesson Four and the Activity for Lesson Four.

2. Teacher's Manual — the Suggested Answers to the Activity for Lesson Four.

MATERIALS

Student book — make copies of Lesson Five and Activities 1 and 2 for Lesson Five to distribute at the end of class.

Classroom Procedure

TIME

1–2 class periods

OBJECTIVES

The students will be able to:

1. Explain what a general warrant was and how and why it was used.
2. Explain the meaning of writs of assistance and how they were used.
3. Explain why there was opposition to the general warrant.
4. Explain what state constitutional provisions regarding warrants were the forerunners of the Fourth Amendment.

MOTIVATION

Ask the students, "Do you know what a warrant is? Do you know what warrants are used for? Today we will discuss the historical origins of warrants."

DEVELOPMENT

1. Discuss students' answers to the Activity for Lesson Four.
2. Use the questions in the activity to help guide students' discussion.
3. For reinforcement, write the key facts on the board or overhead.
4. Distribute and discuss the assignment for Lesson Five.

STUDENT ASSIGNMENT FOR THE NEXT LESSON

Have the students read Lesson Five and do Activities 1 and 2 for Lesson Five. You may want to make this two assignments.

Suggested Answers

ACTIVITY FOR LESSON FOUR

Questions 1–5

1. The general warrant was an order signed by a judge which gave permission to the king's agents to search. They were empowered to search wherever they wanted without having to search for anything specific.

2. The general warrant was used for several purposes: 1) to enforce the payment of custom duties (taxes); 2) to search for and capture criminals; 3) to discourage poaching; 4) to look for stolen goods.

3. Writs of assistance were a type of general warrant signed by a judge. They allowed government agents to force peace officers and ordinary citizens nearby to help them carry out their duties.

4. Opposition to the general warrant grew in England because, since Magna Carta in 1215, the English came to believe that there were certain things a government did not have the right to do to its people. For example, government agents did not have the right to enter a home without a very good reason, and when they did, they should have a specific warrant stating who and/or what they were searching for.

   Opposition to the general warrant grew in the American colonies for the same reasons it grew in England. In addition, the colonists felt that the general warrant was another way in which the government of England sought to oppress them.

5. The Massachusetts Constitution had a provision which prohibited the use of general searches and seizures. Other provisions allowed a warrant to be issued only if the request was backed by an oath or affirmation and the warrant stated exactly who or what to search for.

   The constitutions of Virginia, Pennsylvania, Delaware, and New Hampshire also had provisions which outlawed general warrants or unreasonable searches and seizures.

LESSON FIVE: THE FOURTH AMENDMENT TODAY

Teacher Preparation

READ / REVIEW
1. Student book — Lesson Five and Activities 1 and 2 for Lesson Five. Also review Lesson Four.

2. Teacher's manual — the Suggested Answers to Activities 1 and 2 for Lesson Five. Also review the comment for Case 1: *Terry v. Ohio* (following the answers to the Guide for Analyzing Cases) which discusses reasonable suspicion and probable cause.

MATERIALS
Student book — make copies of Activities 1 and 2 for Lesson Six to distribute at the end of class.

Classroom Procedure

TIME
2 class periods

OBJECTIVES
The students will be able to:
1. Identify the ways in which the Fourth Amendment protects people today.

2. Discuss some circumstances in which frisks or searches can be made without violating the Fourth Amendment.

3. Define legal terms that apply to the Fourth Amendment.

4. Discuss some general guidelines used by judges to determine whether the Fourth Amendment has been violated.

5. Act as judges in deciding cases involving stop and frisk, reasonable expectation of privacy, personal rights, and probable cause.

MOTIVATION
Tell the class, "Today we will discuss some legal procedures that are often confusing and see how they relate to rights guaranteed by the Fourth Amendment."

DEVELOPMENT
1. Put the following question on the board to guide the discussion: What are four areas in which the Fourth Amendment protects people today?

2. List student responses on the board or overhead.

3. Ask the students to give factual situations which involve frisks or searches or hot pursuit by the police that do not violate the Fourth Amendment.

    a. *Terry v. Ohio* would be one example of a stop and frisk.

    b. Another example of a stop and frisk situation would be where a police officer sees a man walking down the street and the officer also sees a bulge which forms the outline of a gun under the man's coat or jacket. The officer would have the right to frisk the person. Once a gun was found, the officer would have probable cause to make an arrest.

    c. An example of hot pursuit would be chasing after a person who has just robbed a store and goes into a building.

4. The students should discuss the meanings of the twelve terms in Activity 1 for Lesson Five.

5. When they have finished discussing the twelve terms, tell the students, "Let's review the way the Fourth Amendment protects people. Often there are alleged violations of people's rights and a judge has to decide if indeed their rights have been violated. We are going to discuss some general guidelines used by judges in determining cases." Make certain that students understand the concepts in Lesson Five B before moving to the next activities.

6. Have students share their definitions of the phrase "a man's home is his castle." Then ask them, "Should the police ever be able to invade the sanctity of the home without a warrant? Under what circumstances would you permit it?"

7. Ask the students to share their definitions of personal rights. Ask students, "If police officers search a home without a warrant and find guns or drugs, and one of the persons arrested and charged with possession of guns or drugs is a visitor, does that person have a right to say his/her Fourth Amendment rights were violated?"

8. Have students share their definitions of reasonable expectation of privacy. Ask them, "If three persons are riding in a car driven by the owner and the police find drugs in the car following an improper search, could the three persons say that they have a reasonable expectation of privacy in the car?"

9. Using examples from the case notebook, explore several situations in which a person has or does not have a reasonable expectation of privacy. Ask the students to act as judges, either individually or in small groups exchanging ideas. Let the students indicate to the class how they would decide the cases if they were judges and have them give their reasons.

10. Ask the students to share their definitions of probable cause. Ask them, "Assume a store has been robbed. How much

information must a police officer have before an arrest can take place? Certainly if the store owner who was robbed pointed out a person, the police would have probable cause. Suppose, however, there is only a description of three men and a description of the car in which they fled. Certainly a police officer would have the right to stop the car. But are there any circumstances short of an identification by the victim under which the police would have probable cause to arrest?"

(The stopping of the car a very short time later and the finding of items stolen from the store might be sufficient probable cause.)

12. As an extending activity, ask one group of students to give some hypothetical-fact situations in which a police officer stops a person and arrests him/her. (Sample cases from the students' notebooks may be used).

Ask a second group of students to act as judges. They should study the facts of the situation and determine if the police officer had probable cause to stop a person or to frisk him.

13. Distribute and discuss the assignment for the next lesson.

STUDENT ASSIGNMENT FOR THE NEXT LESSON

Have the students do Activities 1 and 2 for Lesson Six. You may want to make this two assignments.

Suggested Answers

ACTIVITY 1 FOR LESSON FIVE

Terms 1–12

1. stop and frisk – (stop, question, and search) A police officer may stop and question a person if the officer has reason to believe that the person has committed, is committing, or is about to commit a crime. If the officer fears for his/her safety, s/he may also frisk the person for weapons (pat down the outside of the person's clothing). In a stop and frisk situation, any search must be kept within reasonable bounds.

2. reasonable suspicion – (officer has enough information for assuming a person is doing something wrong) Reasonable suspicion allows an officer to stop and question a suspect. It does not allow the officer to make an arrest.

3. lawful arrest – (officer follows proper arrest procedure based on facts leading to a strong and reasonable belief of suspect's guilt) Making a lawful arrest allows the officer to search a person without a warrant and have him/her

moved to official headquarters. The officer is not allowed to arrest a person without a strong basis for belief in guilt.

4. hot pursuit – (a police officer chasing a suspect, usually right after the commission of a crime) During hot pursuit, a police officer may chase a suspect into areas where s/he could not normally go without a search warrant. The essential elements which make it proper for a police officer to do this are: 1) reasonable or probable cause to believe a crime has been committed and 2) a suspect fleeing in order to escape or avoid arrest.

5. exigent circumstances – (knowledge of dangerous or unlawful activity in a private building that would necessitate an officer entering to stop the activity) Allows an officer to enter a building without a search warrant to prevent dangerous or illegal activity. The officer must have reasonable suspicion, by personal observation or by a reliable informant, that an illegal activity is taking place.

6. consent – (give permission for) An officer can search a person or a building if the person says it is okay. An officer cannot search a person or a home without that person's permission unless she or he has a search warrant.

7. eavesdropping warrant – (legal signed permission to wiretap, place another type of listening device in a private area [such as the wall of a home], or use a videotape) The warrant specifies the suspected crime involved, the person to be listened to, and the type of conversation to be listened for. It allows a tap to be placed on a telephone for reasons specified in the warrant. The tap cannot be placed on any other lines.

8. suppression of evidence – (conceal or prevent the use of evidence at a trial) A judge must prevent evidence from being used in a trial if s/he decides that the evidence was obtained by violating the defendant's Fourth Amendment rights.

9. contraband – (illegal goods such as guns or drugs) Finding illegal goods while using a search warrant permits those goods to be used as evidence in a trial against a person. Finding contraband in an illegal search, however, does not make the search legal.

10. plain view – (out in the open) An officer can seize contraband in plain view even if the search warrant s/he is using does not specify it.

11. good faith – (officers acting on a warrant they think is proper because it was signed by a judge) Officers using a search warrant they think is good allows evidence found to be used in court and the search to be considered legal. The

judge is considered to have made a mistake for signing a warrant without sufficient evidence.

12. exclusionary rule – (disallows evidence seized when Fourth Amendment rights have been violated) The fact that contraband is found during an illegal search doesn't make the search legal. Evidence found under these circumstances must be excluded from a trial.

ACTIVITY 2 FOR LESSON FIVE

Questions 1–4

1. "A man's home is his castle" means, in essence, that a person's home is surrounded by a strong wall of personal rights; therefore, the police should not be able to enter a home unless they have a very good reason.

2. Personal rights are Fourth Amendment rights which a person must claim for him/herself.

3. A reasonable expectation of privacy is the right to privacy which a person has at his/her home, place of business, when talking on the telephone, or in other areas.

   Comment: In the discussion on personal rights and reasonable expectation of privacy, some additional examples might include the following:

   Assume the owner of a house and a visitor are selling drugs. The two people put drugs in the cellar of the house. While the visitor is present, the police come into the house without a warrant and find the drugs. Both the owner of the house and the visitor are arrested for possession of drugs.

   The owner of the house has a reasonable expectation of privacy. S/he can therefore ask a judge to suppress the drugs. Applying the law, the judge would suppress the drugs, and they could not be introduced into evidence at a trial of the owner.

   On the other hand, because Fourth Amendment rights are personal rights, the visitor may have no reasonable expectation of privacy in the house. S/he is merely a visitor. A request to suppress the drugs could therefore be denied by a judge. The drugs could be introduced at the trial, and the visitor could be found guilty of drug possession. Note that the visitor could still argue at trial that s/he knew nothing about the drugs.

   When evidence is suppressed because of a violation of the Fourth Amendment, it cannot be introduced at a trial. Therefore if the only charge against a person is possession of drugs, and the drugs are suppressed, the charge must be dismissed and the person goes free.

4. Probable cause means that a policeman must have strong evidence to believe that a crime is taking place or has taken place before making an arrest.

LESSON SIX, PART I: JUDGE FOR YOURSELF

* NOTE * Lesson Six is divided into four parts in the Teacher's Manual—I–IV. Part I uses Activities 1 and 2 for Lesson Six, Part II uses Activity 3 for Lesson Six, Part III uses Activity 4 for Lesson Six, and Part IV uses Activity 5 for Lesson Six. Completion of these activities will take four to six class periods.

Teacher Preparation

READ / REVIEW
1. Student book — Activities 1 and 2 for Lesson Six. Also, review the cases referenced in Activity 2. In addition, review Lesson Five (The Fourth Amendment Today).

2. Teacher's Manual — the Suggested Answers to Activities 1 and 2 for Lesson Six. Also, review the Teacher's Manual sections which deal with the Activities for Lesson One and Lesson Two.

MATERIALS
Student book — make copies of Activity 3 for Lesson Six to distribute at the end of class.

Classroom Procedure

TIME
1–2 class periods

OBJECTIVES
The students will be able to:
1. Give their opinions about what they believe are the purposes of the Fourth Amendment.

2. Analyze and interpret the facts and holdings of specific cases decided by the Supreme Court.

3. Compare the facts in different cases where similar issues are presented.

4. Discuss and analyze the outcome of particular cases in terms of the different facts in the situations.

MOTIVATION
Tell the students, "We are going to look again at some of the cases that we read before. Now that we have a better understanding of the Fourth Amendment, we are going to compare these cases, decide whether Fourth Amendment rights were violated, and analyze some of their outcomes."

DEVELOPMENT   1. Ask a student to share the answers s/he circled in Activity 1 for Lesson Six (the purposes of the Fourth Amendment). Ask the student why s/he chose those answers. Ask a second student if s/he agrees with the choices made and why. Continue this process with a number of students.

2. The students' answers to Activity 2 for Lesson Six can be shared with the whole class or in small groups. Either way, students should support the reasoning behind their answers. Students with differing viewpoints should state them and support their reasoning. Tell the students that they can use cases from their notebooks to support their answers.

3. Distribute and discuss the assignment for the next lesson.

STUDENT ASSIGNMENT FOR THE NEXT LESSON

Have the students do Activity 3 for Lesson Six (Identification of Exceptions to the Warrant Requirement).

Suggested Answers

ACTIVITY 1 FOR LESSON SIX   The answer to all five questions is "Yes." Make certain that students give reasons for choosing the answers they did.

ACTIVITY 2 FOR LESSON SIX

Interpretation

A. *Terry v. Ohio*

See the Suggested Answers to the Activity for Lesson One.

B. *Terry v. Ohio* and *Sibron v. New York*

1. The officer in *Terry v. Ohio* feared for his safety. We know this because he frisked the suspects for weapons. We know that the officer in *Sibron* did not fear for his safety because he did not frisk the suspect for weapons.

2. No. Even though the officer saw the man talking with several drug addicts over a period of many hours, he did not hear their conversations or see any exchanges of drugs and/or money. He had no reasonable suspicion—sufficient to forcibly stop the man—that the man might be trying to engage in drug sales.

3. The officer in *Terry* followed proper procedure. With reasonable suspicion that a crime was about to be committed, the officer was allowed to stop and question the three men. Because he suspected the men might be planning a robbery and

therefore be armed, he had reason to fear for his safety and frisked the men. When he discovered that two of the men had guns, he proceeded to arrest them for carrying concealed weapons. The third man was not arrested because he did not have a weapon and no crime had yet been committed.

The officer in *Sibron* did not follow proper procedure. Judging from the suspect's behavior (talking to known drug addicts), the officer had an idea that a crime was being or was about to be committed. So it would have been proper for him to stop the man and question him, and if he feared for his safety, to frisk the man for weapons. He did not do this, however. Instead he searched the man immediately, confiscated envelopes containing drugs, then arrested the man. This kind of search for contraband is allowed only after making a legal arrest. The officer did not see the man do anything wrong. He merely saw him talking to known drug addicts and thus he did not have probable cause to make such an arrest. The officer did not question the suspect but rather he searched the suspect improperly. As a result, he did not make a legal arrest.

4. An officer is not allowed to stop and frisk a person unless he or she first has reasonable suspicion that a crime has been, is being, or is about to be committed and also has reason to fear for his or her safety because the person might have a weapon.

C. *Mapp v. Ohio* and *California v. Greenwood*

1. A warrant was required in *Mapp* because the woman had a reasonable expectation of privacy in her home, and there was no evidence that a crime had been, was being, or was about to be committed.

   No warrant was required in *Greenwood* because the garbage had been placed outside of the home on a public curb. Therefore, there was no reasonable expectation of privacy.

2. According to the Supreme Court decision in *California v. Greenwood*, Fourth Amendment protection is lost once the garbage is placed outside the home in a public area. The fact that the garbage might be tied tightly in a bag doesn't change anything.

3. An argument can be made that a person who places garbage at the curb, tightly bound or loosely bound in a garbage can, still has a privacy interest in it and does not want the world to see it. On the other hand, it is simply unrealistic to expect that once items have been discarded at the curb, other persons or animals will not go through it looking for food and other items which might have some value.

D. *Katz v. United States*

1. The Fourth Amendment does not specifically say anything about eavesdropping.

2. The Supreme Court applied the Fourth Amendment to eavesdropping because it said that even though the words of the Fourth Amendment do not explicitly prohibit eavesdropping, the man had a reasonable expectation that his conversations would be private.

3. Before the police or other governmental agencies can wiretap a telephone or eavesdrop in a person's home, they must obtain an eavesdropping warrant that states what crime is involved, the name of the person to be listened to (if known), and what kind of conversation is to be overheard.

4. A reasonable expectation of privacy exists when a person is in a telephone booth because the *person* is involved in this situation, and a person in a home, in a telephone booth, or in other areas has a similar right to privacy.

   No reasonable expectation of privacy exists for garbage placed outside of the home on a public curb because the area is no longer one where privacy can be expected. It should be noted that the issue of discarded garbage and privacy is still being litigated with respect to some state constitutions. Arguments are being made that, even though the Fourth Amendment of the Constitution of the United States does not preclude the police from searching through garbage left in a public place, some state constitutions might well preclude such activity.

E. Exception to the warrant requirement for automobiles

1. An exception is sometimes made to the warrant requirement in the case of automobiles because an automobile can move great distances in a short time, and it would be inconvenient to hold an automobile while a warrant is being obtained.

2. Before an exception to the warrant requirement can be made, an officer must have probable cause that something illegal is in the car.

LESSON SIX, PART II: JUDGE FOR YOURSELF (cont.)

Teacher Preparation

READ / REVIEW
1. Student book — Activity 3 for Lesson Six. Also review Lesson Five.
2. Teacher's manual – the Suggested Answers to Activity 3 for Lesson Six.

MATERIALS
Student book — Make copies of Activity 4 for Lesson Six to distribute at the end of class.

Classroom Procedure

TIME
1 class period

OBJECTIVES
The student will be able to:
1. Identify exceptions to the requirement of a search warrant.
2. Apply these exceptions to specific factual situations.

MOTIVATION
Tell the students, "Today we will review what we have learned about warrants—the normal requirements for using them and any exceptions to these requirements."

DEVELOPMENT
1. Tell the students that they are going to go over the cases from their homework and, in each case, identify the exception to the warrant requirement. They should also indicate why they chose that exception.
2. Ask a student to state the basic facts in Case 1: *Cupp v. Murphy* (they can use the Guide for Analyzing Cases to help them with this). Have another student identify which exception to the warrant requirement applies and why. If there is any disagreement, make certain that students support their reasoning.
3. Go over the remaining three cases, repeating the process they used for Case 1.
4. Distribute and discuss the assignment for the next lesson.

**STUDENT
ASSIGNMENT
FOR THE NEXT
LESSON**

Have the students do Activity 4 for Lesson Six. Since there are
nine cases involved, you may want to make this two assignments.

Suggested Answers

**ACTIVITY 3 FOR
LESSON SIX**

**Identification of Exceptions to the Warrant Requirement
Case 1: *Cupp v. Murphy*, 412 U.S. 291 (1973)**

Answer: c. exigent circumstances accompanied by probable
cause

(The Supreme Court ruled that the search was proper. The
Court said that Murphy could have destroyed the fingernail
evidence if it had not been forcibly removed at the time he
appeared at the police station.)

Case 2: *United States v. Mendenhall*, 446 U.S. 544 (1980)

Answer: a. consent

(The Supreme Court held that the stop was permissible
under standards set out in *Terry v. Ohio*. It also ruled that
Mendenhall gave a valid consent to the search.)

**Case 3: *Warden, Maryland Penitentiary v. Hayden*,
387 U.S. 294 (1967)**

Answer: d. hot pursuit

(The Supreme Court ruled that the entry and search by the
police was proper. The police were in hot pursuit of a fleeing
suspect.)

Case 4: *Pennsylvania v. Mimms*, 434 U.S. 106 (1977)

Answer: e. stop and frisk

(The Supreme Court of the United States ruled that the stop
and frisk of Mimms was proper. The car had an expired
license plate, and this was a valid reason to stop it. When the
officer saw the bulge and feared for his safety, he had a valid
reason to frisk Mimms.)

LESSON SIX, PART III: JUDGE FOR YOURSELF (cont.)

Teacher Preparation

READ / REVIEW
1. Student book — Activity 4 for Lesson Six.
2. Teacher's manual — the Suggested Answers to Activity 4 for Lesson Six.

MATERIALS
Student book — make copies of Activity 5 for Lesson six to distribute at the end of class.

Classroom Procedure

TIME
1–2 class periods

OBJECTIVES
The students will be able to:
1. Apply the knowledge they have learned in this unit.
2. Use critical thinking skills such as evaluating, comparing, contrasting, analyzing, inferring, and evaluating to make decisions about several cases.

MOTIVATION
Tell the students, "For this activity you will act as judges. You will analyze several cases and decide how the Fourth Amendment should be applied in these cases."

DEVELOPMENT
1. Activity 4 for Lesson 6 is a culmination of this unit. The students will apply the knowledge they have learned and use critical thinking skills to judge a series of new cases.
2. Use a variety of group situations in order to allow students opportunities to interact and share ideas about the cases.
3. When the students have finished working in their groups, they can share and discuss their answers with the class.
5. Distribute and discuss the assignment for the next lesson.

STUDENT ASSIGNMENT FOR THE NEXT LESSON
Have the students do Activity 5 for Lesson Six.

Suggested Answers

ACTIVITY 4 FOR LESSON SIX

Judging a Variety of Cases
Case 1: *New Jersey v. T.L.O.*, 469 U.S. 325 (1985)

The Supreme Court of the United States ruled that the Fourth Amendment does apply to searches made by school officials. It further ruled that no search warrant was necessary in this case. No probable cause standard had to be met. Instead, the standard was whether the search was reasonable under the circumstances. Here the Supreme Court upheld the search as reasonable.

Comment: Basically these questions seek to determine whether the students feel there is something about a school setting which should cause a relaxation of the Fourth Amendment. Ordinarily under the Fourth Amendment, a search of a person or of his/her effects would not be permitted in the absence of circumstances discussed in the text (a lawful arrest, stop and frisk, etc.).

In response to any questions regarding T.L.O.'s right to privacy, the court's decision in this case stated that there is a right to privacy among students. However, there is a need to strike a "balance between the schoolchild's legitimate expectations of privacy and the school's equally legitimate need to maintain an environment in which learning can take place." (469 U.S. at p. 340)

Case 2: *Mincey v. Arizona*, 437 U.S. 385 (1978)

The Supreme Court ruled that the search violated the Fourth Amendment. The fact that a murder scene was involved did not create an emergency situation that justified a warrantless search. The fact that drugs were involved made no difference in the need for a warrant to search the entire premises.

Comment: Even though a murder had been committed, a search warrant should be obtained to search the premises. The officers could, however, without a warrant, make an inspection of the place to make sure they were not in danger. Moreover, they could secure the premises, that is, prevent anyone from disturbing or moving anything while a warrant was obtained.

Case 3: *Chimel v. California*, 395 U.S. 752 (1969)

The Supreme Court ruled that in order to search the house, a warrant was necessary. The police could make a limited search in the area near the arrested person to make sure he did not obtain a weapon. It suppressed the evidence seized in the search of the house.

Comment: An arrest warrant is not an authorization to search a premises. The officers would have to have a warrant authorizing a search of the premises in addition to a warrant to arrest a person.

Case 4: *Stanford v. Texas*, 379 U.S. 476 (1965)

The Supreme Court ruled that the search was a violation of the Fourth Amendment because the search warrant issued was a general warrant which the Fourth Amendment forbids.

Comment: The reasoning of the court was that the warrant used was a general warrant because it did not specify which books, records, pamphlets, etc. to seize.

Case 5: *Ker v. California*, 374 U.S. 23 (1963)

The Supreme Court affirmed the convictions. It held that the police had probable cause to arrest George Ker when they entered the apartment. It also ruled that Diane Ker's arrest was justified because marijuana was in plain view in the kitchen.

Comment: While the police may have had probable cause to arrest George Ker when they went to his home, the law now requires that the police obtain an arrest warrant in order to arrest a person in the home in the absence of exigent circumstances (e.g., a robber fleeing into a home). (*Payton v. New York*, 445 U.S. 574 [1980]) Therefore, if the police today went to the home without a warrant and arrested Ker for drugs, the drugs found would have to be suppressed. Assuming, however, that the officers had an arrest warrant for a person but not a search warrant for the home, they could still seize any contraband (drugs, guns) in plain view at the time of the arrest.

Case 6: *O'Connor v. Ortega*, 480 U.S. 709 (1987)

The Supreme Court held that no warrant was necessary to search the office and desk. The office and desk could be searched if there was a reasonable basis for doing so.

Comment: In this case the Supreme Court concluded that the search might be reasonable under the circumstances. It remanded the case for a determination of the circumstances of the search. The case was decided by a 5 to 4 vote. The dissenters concluded that Dr. Ortega had a reasonable expectation of privacy in his office and that the search violated the Fourth Amendment. Note that the decision involved only public (governmental) employees; therefore, their actions had to be viewed in terms of Fourth Amendment constraints on governmental action.

Case 7: *Hudson v. Palmer*, 468 U.S. 517 (1984)

The Supreme Court held that there was no right to privacy in a prison cell. The search was proper.

Comment: When a person is in prison, because of security measures and the difficulties of administering a prison, privacy rights ordinarily available to a citizen may be diminished.

Case 8: *Schmerber v. California*, 384 U.S. 757 (1966)

The Supreme Court ruled that no violation of the Fourth Amendment had occurred. One of the reasons for permitting the test was the fact that it had to be done quickly since there was probable cause to believe the defendant was intoxicated, and evidence of intoxication would disappear with time. This was a case of exigent circumstances.

Case 9: *Massachusetts v. Sheppard*, 468 U.S. 981 (1984)

The Supreme Court upheld the search. It stated that the police officers relied in good faith on the judge's signature and the judge's statement to them that the search warrant was proper.

Comment: This case presents facts which clearly show that a mistake was made. The police officers went to the judge to get a warrant in order to search for evidence of a murder. The judge apparently thought he had issued a warrant to search for evidence of a murder. The warrant, a form which directed a search for drugs, was not properly changed by the judge. The Supreme Court permitted a good faith exception to the warrant requirement. It allowed the evidence of the murder found in the search to be used even though the warrant mistakenly said to search for drugs.

LESSON SIX, PART IV: JUDGE FOR YOURSELF (cont.)

Teacher Preparation

READ / REVIEW   1. Student book — Activity 5 for Lesson Six.

2. Teacher's manual — the Suggested Answers to Activity 5 for Lesson Six.

MATERIALS   None needed for homework. The first lesson of Chapter Three (The Fifth & Sixth Amendments) will be an in-class activity.

Classroom Procedure

TIME   1 class period

OBJECTIVES   Using their knowledge of the Fourth Amendment, the students should be able to give reasons why they believe drug testing of the occupations listed should or should not be undertaken without reasonable suspicion.

MOTIVATION   Tell the students, "Drug testing is a type of search. Under a limited set of circumstances, drug testing may be required without reasonable suspicion. Under most circumstances, there must be some reasonable suspicion of drug use before a state or governmental body can order drug testing."

DEVELOPMENT   1. Divide the students into five groups and have each group consider three of the occupations listed. The group should discuss reasons why drug testing of those occupations, without reasonable suspicion, should or should not be required. Then the group should decide, as judges, whether to permit the testing.

2. The groups should report their discussions and conclusions to the entire group.

STUDENT ASSIGNMENT FOR THE NEXT LESSON   The next lesson is an in-class assignment.

Suggested Answers

ACTIVITY 5 FOR
LESSON SIX

Testing for Drugs

This activity asks students to state their opinions and to give reasons for their answers. There are no right or wrong answers, but the following information can be used if students need help with their reasoning and their discussions.

There are some jobs in which drug testing may be required even though there are no apparent signs of and no reasonable suspicion of drug use. These jobs include airline pilots because of the dangers in flying. They may also include police officers who are assigned to units engaged in fighting drug activity because of the nature of their work.

There are some circumstances in which drug testing may be required without visible signs of drug use. Thus train or bus engineers or drivers may be automatically tested following an accident to see if drugs played any part in the accident.

At other times and in other circumstances, some reasonable suspicion of drug usage might be necessary before drug testing could be required. For example, a person (a teacher, fireman, or other employee) who came to work with slurred speech, a runny nose, and a drowsy appearance might be required to undergo a drug test. Testing in these instances would be based on reasonable suspicion.

CHAPTER THREE: THE FIFTH & SIXTH AMENDMENTS
LESSON ONE: YOU BE THE JUDGE

Teacher Preparation

READ/REVIEW
1. Student book — Lesson One and the Activity for Lesson One. Also read Lesson Six D for background.

2. Teacher's manual — the Suggested Answers to the Activity for Lesson One.

MATERIALS
Student book — make copies of Lesson One and the Activity for Lesson One for this class period. Also make copies of Lesson Two (What Does the Fifth Amendment Say?) and the Activity for Lesson Two to distribute at the end of class.

Classroom Procedure

TIME
1–2 class periods

OBJECTIVES
The students will be able to:

1. Discuss what is meant by, "I plead the Fifth."

2. Analyze cases and decide whether the defendants' rights were violated.

MOTIVATION
Tell the students, "We are going to look at the Fifth and Sixth Amendments in this chapter. Lesson One contains two cases that are related to the Fifth Amendment."

DEVELOPMENT
1. Ask the students if they have ever heard the expression, "I plead the Fifth." If so, ask them where they heard it and what they think it means. (The students may discuss television shows where courtroom scenes were shown.)

2. Now divide the students into groups of 5 or 6 and assign each group one of the two cases in Lesson One.

3. Give each group a copy of the Guide for Analyzing Cases to fill out for their assigned case. Each group should appoint someone to record their information.

4. After the students have discussed the cases and filled out their Guides, they should come back together as a large group to discuss the cases and answer questions 1–4 in the Activity for Lesson One.

5. Distribute and discuss the assignment for Lesson Two.

STUDENT ASSIGNMENT FOR THE NEXT LESSON

Have the students read Lesson Two (What Does the Fifth Amendment Say?) and do the Activity for Lesson Two.

Suggested Answers

ACTIVITY FOR LESSON ONE

Case 1: *Brown v. Mississippi*, 297 U.S. 278 (1936) – Guide for Analyzing Cases

1. The main facts of the case are:
   a. Three persons were arrested and tried for the murder of another person.
   b. All three confessed, were found guilty, and were sentenced to death.
   c. Without their confessions, there would have been insufficient evidence to convict them. The judge would have had to dismiss the case.
   d. One of the defendants, a man named Ellington, was temporarily hung and beaten twice by some white men who wanted him to confess to the crime. He did not confess and was released.
   e. Two days later he was arrested and beaten again by the deputy sheriff. He then agreed to confess and named two other persons, Ed Brown and Henry Shields.
   f. Brown and Shields were also arrested and beaten until they confessed.
   g. The confessions were introduced at their trial.
   h. Their main defense was that their confessions had been coerced.
   i. The deputy sheriff and others admitted the beatings.

2. The amendment involved is the Fifth Amendment.

3. Information not given. (The Right Against Self-Incrimination Clause was involved.)

4. The men were accused of violating a state law prohibiting murder.

5. Information not given. (The issue was whether these defendants were forced to incriminate themselves. In other words, did they confess because they were beaten?)

6. Information not given. (The Supreme Court reversed the convictions of the defendants.)

7. Information not given. (The Supreme Court reversed the convictions because the confessions were coerced [beaten] out of the defendants.)

Answers to Questions 1 and 2 – *Brown v. Mississippi***:**
Since the confessions in Brown were beaten out of the defendants, they should not have been admitted. A confession beaten and coerced from a person is inherently unreliable. A person who is beaten may confess simply to escape further beating. Because of the unreliability of coerced confessions, a person should not be convicted if the main evidence is that confession.

Comment: *Brown v. Mississippi*, as well as *Powell v. Alabama* (Chapter Three, Lesson Seven I of the student book), are cases involving black defendants accused of crimes against whites in the South in the 1930s. If students ask why the defendants in these cases received the treatment they did, explain that one reason was because of their race. In both cases, the fact of race was convincingly made in the Supreme Court decisions.

Case 2: *California v. Stewart***, 384 U.S. 436 (1966) –**
Guide for Analyzing Cases
1. The main facts of the case are:
    a. A series of robberies occurred in Los Angeles, California.
    b. During one of these robberies a person was assaulted and she later died of her injuries.
    c. The defendant in the case, Stewart, was seen cashing a dividend check taken in one of the robberies.
    d. Stewart was arrested at his home along with his wife and three other persons who were there.
    e. Police asked if they could search the house and Stewart consented.
    f. The police found items taken from several robberies.
    g. Stewart was arrested and questioned nine times over five days. Except for the first questioning, when an accusing witness was present, he was alone with his interrogators.
    h. During the ninth questioning, Stewart admitted the robbery of the person who died.
    i. Stewart was taken before a magistrate and held for trial. The four other persons were released.

2. The amendment involved is the Fifth Amendment.

3. Information not given. (The Right Against Self-Incrimination Clause is involved.)

4. The state laws allegedly violated included laws against kidnapping to commit murder, robbery, and rape.

5. Information not given. (The issue was whether the arrest or conviction of the defendant violated the Right Against Self-Incrimination Clause of the Fifth Amendment.)

6. Information not given. (The Supreme Court reversed Stewart's conviction.)

7. Information not given. (The Supreme Court was concerned that individuals be given protection against self-incrimination. The Court decided that any suspect who is in custody or undergoing custodial interrogation must be given four warnings which are called the "Miranda warnings." We will study these warnings in Lesson Six, The Fifth Amendment Today.)

Answers to Questions 3 and 4 – *California v. Stewart*:
California v. Stewart was one of four cases decided by the Supreme Court in *Miranda v. Arizona*. As stated previously, the Supreme Court announced the four Miranda warnings in that case. Although there was no evidence of physical beatings in the cases decided in *Miranda*, the Supreme Court was concerned about psychological coercion. This meant that a person who was in a police-dominated setting might have his/her will to resist overcome. The person might confess because of the police atmosphere. If this reasoning is followed, the confession in *Stewart* should not be admitted, and a defendant should not be convicted when the main evidence is his confession. It should be noted, however, that *Miranda* was a five to four decision and one that was extremely controversial. There are still a number of people who, even though they abide by the *Miranda* decision because it is the law, believe that no warnings should be given. Alerting a defendant in accordance with *Miranda*, they argue, is a hindrance to law enforcement.

LESSON TWO: WHAT DOES THE FIFTH AMENDMENT SAY?

Teacher Preparation

READ/REVIEW   1. Student book — Lesson Two and the Activity for Lesson Two.

2. Teacher's manual — the Suggested Answers to the Activity for Lesson Two.

MATERIALS   Student book — make copies of Lesson Three (What Does the Sixth Amendment Say?) and the Activity for Lesson Three to distribute at the end of class.

Classroom Procedure

TIME   1 class period

OBJECTIVES   The students will be able to:

1. State what they believe the words of the Fifth Amendment mean.

2. Identify and explain what rights the Fifth Amendment grants.

MOTIVATION   Tell the students, "In this lesson we will look at the wording of the Fifth Amendment and identify which of our rights it guarantees."

DEVELOPMENT   1. Go over the Activity for Lesson Two, giving several students an opportunity to read the choices they made as alternatives to the words or phrases in the Fifth Amendment. Ask them why they made these choices. Any choice is acceptable as long as a student can support his/her choice. Be certain that students understand all of the vocabulary.

2. Ask one student to read his/her interpretation of what the Fifth Amendment means. Ask if other students have significantly different meanings. If so, ask them to support their reasoning.

3. Have the students identify the various rights guaranteed by the Fifth Amendment. If desired, note these on the board or overhead. Make certain they address the following key points:

      — prosecution for a capital or other serious crime only after indictment by a grand jury except for the armed forces or militia in time of war

      — no double jeopardy

      — no self-incrimination

      — no deprivation of life, liberty, or property without due process of law.

4. Distribute and discuss the assignment for Lesson Three.

STUDENT ASSIGNMENT FOR THE NEXT LESSON

Have the students read Lesson Three (What Does the Sixth Amendment Say?) and do the Activity for Lesson Three.

Suggested Answers

ACTIVITY FOR LESSON TWO

Below are the most appropriate choices from the three alternatives provided. Be prepared to accept students' other choices as long as they are able to support their choices.

1. punishable by death
2. wicked
3. statement
4. legal accusation
5. group which formally charges
6. citizens subject to being called to the military in an emergency
7. tried
8. crime
9. at risk
10. forced
11. denied
12. lawful procedures
13. payment

LESSON THREE: WHAT DOES THE SIXTH AMENDMENT SAY?

Teacher Preparation

READ / REVIEW

1. Student book — Lesson Three and the Activity for Lesson Three.

2. Teacher's manual — the Suggested Answers to the Activity for Lesson Three.

MATERIALS

Student book — make copies of Lesson Four and the Activity for Lesson Four to distribute at the end of class.

Classroom Procedure

TIME

1 class period

OBJECTIVES

The students will be able to:

1. State what they believe the words of the Sixth Amendment mean.

2. Identify and explain what rights the Sixth Amendment grants.

MOTIVATION

Tell the students, "In this lesson we will examine the wording of the Sixth Amendment to see how it guarantees our right to a fair trial."

DEVELOPMENT

1. Go over the Activity for Lesson Three, giving several students an opportunity to read the choices they made as alternatives to the words or phrases in the Sixth Amendment. Ask them why they made these choices and to tell their reasons. Be certain that students understand all of the vocabulary.

2. Ask a student to read his/her interpretation of what the Sixth Amendment means. Ask if other students have significantly different meanings. If so, ask them to support their reasoning.

3. Have the students identify the various rights guaranteed by the Sixth Amendment. If desired, note these on the board or overhead. Make certain they address the following key points:

- a speedy and public trial
- an impartial jury
- to be informed of the nature and cause of the accusation
- confrontation with witnesses
- compulsory process for obtaining witnesses in defendant's favor
- assistance of counsel for defense.

4. Distribute and discuss the assignment for Lesson Four.

STUDENT ASSIGNMENT FOR THE NEXT LESSON

Lesson Four contains four cases that are related to the Fifth and Sixth Amendments. You may want to divide the cases for study. The first two cases (Double Jeopardy and Involuntary Confessions) are related to the Fifth Amendment. These could be studied for one class. The next two cases (Right to a Jury Trial and Right to Confront Witnesses) are related to the Sixth Amendment and could be studied for the next class. The students should use the Guide for Analyzing Cases to aid in their understanding of the cases and write their answers to the Guide questions for class discussion purposes.

Suggested Answers

ACTIVITY FOR LESSON THREE

Given below are the most appropriate choices from the three alternatives provided. Be prepared to accept students' other choices as long as they are able to support their choices.

1. lawsuits, actions
2. defendant
3. fair
4. performed
5. determined
6. charge
7. faced
8. a court order requiring attendance
9. persons who may have evidence of a crime or have evidence tending to show non-guilt
10. a lawyer
11. protection

LESSON FOUR: SOME PAST DECISIONS OF THE SUPREME COURT

Teacher Preparation

READ / REVIEW
1. Student book — Lesson Four and the Activity for Lesson Four.

2. Teacher's manual — the Suggested Answers to the Activity for Lesson Four.

MATERIALS   Student book — make copies of Lesson Five and the Activity for Lesson Five to distribute at the end of class.

Classroom Procedure

TIME   1 class period

OBJECTIVES   The students will be able to:

1. Apply the knowledge they have learned about Fifth and Sixth Amendment rights to four cases.

2. Analyze the facts stated in the cases and state whether they agree with the decisions of the Supreme Court.

3. Communicate their ideas in small and large group settings.

MOTIVATION   Tell the students, "We have studied the Fifth and Sixth Amendments and the rights they guarantee. Now we are going to look at four cases that involve Fifth and Sixth Amendment issues."

DEVELOPMENT
1. The students were assigned the four cases in Lesson Four. Two of the cases deal with the Fifth Amendment and two cases deal with the Sixth Amendment.

2. Divide the students into four groups and assign one case to each group. Have each group discuss their assigned case and fill out a new Guide from the responses they gave in their homework.

3. Have the students come back together as a whole class. Have one person from each group identify the facts and issues of their case. If desired, highlight the points of each case on the board or overhead.

4. Have each group indicate whether they agree with the Supreme Court decision in their case and give their reasons. If they do not agree, ask them to state how and for what reasons they would decide the case differently. When each group has finished, open the discussion to the rest of the class.

5. If students are having difficulty understanding vocabulary such as *felony*, *misdemeanor*, *burglary*, *robbery*, and *larceny*, allow time for them to investigate and discuss the meanings of and differences between these terms.

6. Distribute and discuss the assignment for Lesson Five.

STUDENT ASSIGNMENT FOR THE NEXT LESSON

Have the students read Lesson Five (What Are the Origins of Some of the Rights Guaranteed by the Fifth and Sixth Amendments?) and do the Activity for Lesson Five.

Suggested Answers

ACTIVITY FOR LESSON ONE

Cases 1–4

Case 1: Double Jeopardy—*Benton v. Maryland*, 395 U.S. 784 (1969) – Guide for Analyzing Cases

1. The main facts of the case are:
   a. The defendant was tried in a Maryland state court for burglary and larceny.
   b. He was found guilty of burglary but not guilty of larceny.
   c. He appealed the burglary conviction, but before his appeal could be heard, a ruling in another case said that a provision of the state constitution was invalid. The invalid provision required a juror to state his or her belief in God.
   d. The jurors in the Benton case had had to declare their belief in God. Because they should not have been forced to do so, Benton's conviction was overturned (reversed) and the case was sent back to the lower court for a new trial on both offences.
   e. Benton protested that he should not be tried again for both burglary and larceny, but he was tried for both and found guilty of both.
   f. Benton appealed to the state appellate court saying that his conviction violated the Double Jeopardy Clause of the Fifth Amendment. His appeal was denied and the case went to the U.S. Supreme Court.

2. The Amendment involved was the Fifth Amendment.

3. The Double Jeopardy Clause was involved.

4. The state laws allegedly violated prohibited burglary and larceny.

5. The issue was whether Benton's conviction of larceny the second time he was tried was a violation of the Double Jeopardy Clause of the Fifth Amendment.

6. The Supreme Court reversed the defendant's conviction for larceny at his second trial.

7. The Supreme Court ruled that the Double Jeopardy Clause of the Fifth Amendment applied to the states through the Due Process Clause of the Fourteenth Amendment. (Benton could not be tried a second time for the same offense after being found not guilty the first time.)

Case 2: Involuntary Confessions—*Mincey v. Arizona*, 437 U.S. 385 (1978) – Guide for Analyzing Cases
1. The main facts of the case are:
   a. There was a narcotics raid on an apartment.
   b. The defendant, Mincey, was severely wounded and an undercover police officer was shot and killed.
   c. Mincey was taken to a hospital where a detective came to question him. Because Mincey had tubes in his throat, he had to respond to questions in writing.
   d. Mincey stated that he wanted a lawyer, but the detective told him he was under arrest for murder and continued to question him about the events at the apartment.
   e. At the trial, Mincey's written answers were not used in the prosecution's direct case against him. However, when Mincey took the stand and testified, the prosecutor used the written answers to attempt to impeach him (show he was not believable because he said something different at the hospital).

2. The Amendment involved was the Fifth Amendment.

3. The Clause Against Self-Incrimination was involved.

4. The state law which was allegedly violated prohibited murder.

5. The issue was whether the statements made by the defendant at the hospital were voluntary.

6. The Supreme Court decided that the use of the statements was a violation of due process of law.

7. The Supreme Court said that because of the defendant's condition, he could not exercise his free will in responding. The Court ruled that the statements at the hospital were not voluntary.

Case 3: Right to a Jury Trial—*Duncan v. Louisiana*, 391 U.S. 145 (1968) – Guide for Analyzing Cases
1. The main facts of the case are:
   a. A 19–year-old man, Duncan, was tried and convicted of simple battery.
   b. He was found guilty of slapping another person on the elbow after seeing his two cousins talking to four white boys. This was after his cousins had recently transferred to an all-white school and had reported racial incidents there.
   c. Duncan was sentenced to jail for 60 days and fined $150.
   d. He requested a jury trial but the request was denied since Louisiana law permitted a jury trial only in cases involving capital punishment or imprisonment at hard labor.
   e. Duncan appealed his conviction to the Supreme Court.

2. The Sixth Amendment is involved.

3. The Right to a Jury Trial Clause is involved.

4. The state statute the defendant was alleged to have violated prohibited battery and authorized imprisonment for up to two years if a person was convicted.

5. The issue was whether the Louisiana law violated the right to a jury trial.

6. The Supreme Court reversed the conviction of the defendant.

7. The Supreme Court held that the right to a jury trial was guaranteed by the Sixth and Fourteenth Amendments to the Constitution in all cases involving serious crimes.

Comment: Duncan was never retried. When the case was reversed by the Supreme Court, Duncan brought an action in the United States District Court for the Eastern District of Louisiana seeking to enjoin (stop) the retrial. The District Court enjoined the reprosecution (*Duncan v. Perez*, 321 F. Supp. 181 [1970]). On appeal the United States Court of Appeals, Fifth Circuit affirmed the decision of the district court. The Fifth Circuit agreed with the district court and ruled that the state attorney was prosecuting the case in bad faith and for harassment. It further ruled that any prosecution of Duncan would deter blacks in that part of Louisiana from exercising their rights (to school desegregation, etc.). (*Duncan v. Perez*, 445 F. 2d 557 [1971])

Case 4: Right to Confront Witnesses—*Pointer v. Texas*, 380 U.S. 400 (1965) – Guide for Analyzing Cases
1. The main facts of the case are:

    a. Two people were arrested for the robbery of a third person.

    b. At a preliminary hearing the victim testified to the robbery.

    c. The defendants had no lawyers and did not cross-examine the victim.

    d. The victim then moved from the state.

    e. At the trial, the prosecutor tried to introduce the testimony of the victim given at the preliminary hearing.

    f. One of the defendants, Pointer, objected on the grounds that he had not cross-examined the victim at the preliminary hearing.

    g. His objection was overruled and he was convicted.

    h. He appealed his case to the highest court for criminal appeals in Texas. That court upheld his conviction.

    i. His case then went to the Supreme Court.

2. The Amendment involved is the Sixth Amendment.

3. The Confrontation Clause is involved.

4. The state law allegedly violated prohibited the robbery of another person.

5. The issue or problem was whether the conviction violated the Confrontation Clause.

6. The Supreme Court reversed the conviction and remanded (returned) the case to the Texas courts for further proceedings.

7. The Supreme Court held that the Confrontation Clause of the Sixth Amendment applied to the states through the Due Process Clause of the Fourteenth Amendment. It further held that the right to confrontation had been violated.

Comment on Cases 1–4: As we read in Chapter One, until the Twentieth Century, the Supreme Court of the United States ruled that the Bill of Rights was a check on the federal government but not the state governments. During the time that Earl Warren was Chief Justice (1953–1969), the Supreme Court made almost all of the rights in the Bill of Rights applicable to the states. A part of each of the Supreme Court rulings in the four cases was to state that certain rights were applicable to the states. These rights were: no double jeopardy (*Benton v. Maryland*), a right against self-incrimination (*Mincey v. Arizona*), the right to a jury trial (*Duncan v. Louisiana*), and the right to confront witnesses (*Pointer v. Texas*).

LESSON FIVE: WHAT ARE THE ORIGINS OF SOME OF THE RIGHTS GUARANTEED BY THE FIFTH AND SIXTH AMENDMENTS?

Teacher Preparation

READ / REVIEW

1. Student book — Lesson Five and the Activity for Lesson Five.

2. Teacher's manual — the Suggested Answers to the Activity for Lesson Five.

MATERIALS

Student book — make copies of Lesson Six (The Fifth Amendment Today) and Activities 1 and 2 for Lesson Six to distribute at the end of class.

Classroom Procedure

TIME

1 class period

OBJECTIVES

The students will be able to:

1. Identify the origins of some of the rights guaranteed by the Fifth and Sixth Amendments.

2. Review the steps involved in the adoption of the Bill of Rights.

MOTIVATION

Tell the students, "Today we are going to discuss the historical origins of the Fifth and Sixth Amendments."

DEVELOPMENT

1. Use the questions in the Activity for Lesson Five to guide the discussion. Students can use the answers they wrote for this lesson to aid their discussion.

2. Question Six in the Activity for Lesson Five asks students to review the steps for the adoption of the Bill of Rights. Ask the students to verbalize these steps and write them on the board or on an overhead.

3. Distribute and discuss the assignment for Lesson Six.

STUDENT ASSIGNMENT FOR THE NEXT LESSON

Have the students read Lesson Six (The Fifth Amendment Today) and do Activities 1 and 2 for Lesson Six.

Suggested Answers

ACTIVITY FOR LESSON FIVE

Questions 1–6

1. Most of the rights guaranteed by the Fifth and Sixth Amendments came directly from England (some dated back at least to ancient Greece and Rome).

2. Those who were attacked for being outside of the mainstream of religious belief often did not wish to reveal their innermost thoughts. In addition, the right against self-incrimination came to be one of the rights which Englishmen insisted the monarchy could not take away. It was a shield against torture and coerced confessions.

3. John Lilburne's case was significant to the Fifth Amendment because during his trial Lilburne refused to give any evidence which might incriminate himself. Following his case, the right to a public trial was made a part of English law and, subsequently, part of the Sixth Amendment.

4. Citizens in England felt that a trial by jury would insure fairness. A jury trial meant that the king could not arbitrarily decide a person's guilt. This was a decision that citizens felt could only be made by a person's peers.

5. Virginia had provisions protecting freedom of religion and the press as well as provisions similar to those found in the Fourth, Fifth, Sixth, and Eighth Amendments. Pennsylvania had provisions protecting freedom of speech, religion, and the right to counsel in criminal cases. Massachusetts had provisions forbidding unreasonable searches and seizures.

6. See the student book (Chapter One, Lesson Six D) and the teacher's manual (Chapter One, Lesson Six) for information about the adoption of the Bill of Rights.

LESSON SIX: THE FIFTH AMENDMENT TODAY

Teacher Preparation

READ / REVIEW
1. Student book—Lesson Six and Activities 1 and 2 for Lesson Six.

2. Teacher's manual—the Suggested Answers to Activities 1 and 2 for Lesson Six.

MATERIALS
Student book — make copies of Lesson Seven (The Sixth Amendment Today) and Activities 1–3 for Lesson Seven to distribute at the end of class.

Classroom Procedure

TIME
1–2 class periods

OBJECTIVES
The students will be able to:

1. Explain the key rights in the Fifth Amendment in more detail and discuss how they are applied to contemporary cases.

2. Understand the Miranda warnings and learn when they apply.

MOTIVATION
Tell the students, "Lesson Six deals with the rights guaranteed by the Fifth Amendment. These rights involve some complicated concepts. We need to discuss each of these concepts in order to better understand all that the Fifth Amendment entails."

DEVELOPMENT
1. For this lesson, each student was to write one or two sentences to explain the meaning of the key rights given under the Fifth Amendment.

2. Engage the students in a discussion about these key rights:
   – indictment
   – grand jury
   – double jeopardy
   – "taking the Fifth" (right against self-incrimination)
   – due process
   List these rights on the board.

3. Use the following questions to help focus the discussion:
   a. What is the role of a grand jury?
   b. Can a person be tried twice for a crime? Why or why not?
   c. What does the phrase "taking the Fifth" mean? Can a person accused of any crime "take the Fifth"?
   d. Does a defendant have to testify during a trial? Who must prove a person guilty?
   e. Can a confession be coerced? Recall Case 1 in Lesson One: *Brown v. Mississippi*.
   f. What are the "Miranda warnings"? Recall for discussion Case 2 in Lesson One: *California v. Stewart*.
   g. When must the Miranda warnings be given? What happens if Miranda warnings are not given?
   h. What is due process.

4. Distribute and discuss the assignment for Lesson Seven.

STUDENT ASSIGNMENT FOR THE NEXT LESSON

Have the students read Lesson Seven (The Sixth Amendment Today) and do the Activities for Lesson Seven. You may want to have the students do Activities 1 and 2 for Lesson Seven for one class period and have them do Activity 3 for Lesson Seven for another class period.

Suggested Answers

ACTIVITY 1 FOR LESSON SIX

Terms 1–5

1. indictment – a list of charges drawn when a grand jury votes to begin or to continue formal criminal proceedings against a person accused of a crime.

2. grand jury – a body of citizens that formally looks at evidence in the hands of a prosecutor and decides if there is enough evidence to start or continue formal proceedings against a person accused of a crime.

3. double jeopardy – a person cannot be tried for a crime, found not guilty, and tried again for the same crime. However, if a person is tried and convicted, and his conviction is reversed on appeal, he can be tried again if other evidence is found against him.

4. right against self-incrimination ("taking the Fifth") – a person cannot be forced to testify against himself and thus prove his own guilt.

5. due process – a person's right to a fair legal procedure when s/he is accused of a crime.

ACTIVITY 2 FOR LESSON SIX

Questions 1 and 2

1. Miranda warnings – a procedure police must use when questioning suspects who are in custody in order to protect their Fifth Amendment rights. The four Miranda warnings are:

    a. You have the right to remain silent.

    b. Anything you say may be used against you in a court of law.

    c. You have the right to an attorney.

    d. If you cannot afford an attorney, one will be appointed for you free of charge.

2. Miranda warnings must be given after someone is taken into custody or deprived of freedom in a significant way (that is, not be free to leave the presence of the police) but before interrogation begins.

LESSON SEVEN: THE SIXTH AMENDMENT TODAY

Teacher Preparation

READ / REVIEW   1. Student book — Lesson Seven and Activities 1–3 for Lesson Seven.

2. Teacher's manual — the Suggested Answers to Activities 1–3 for Lesson Seven.

MATERIALS   Student book — make copies of Lesson Eight (Judge for Yourself) and the Activity for Lesson Eight to distribute at the end of class.

Classroom Procedure

TIME   1–2 class periods

OBJECTIVES   The students will be able to:

1. Explain the key rights of the Sixth Amendment in more detail.

2. Discuss the important issues related to the Sixth Amendment and how they relate to contemporary cases.

MOTIVATION   Tell the students, "The Sixth Amendment deals with criminal proceedings. We are going to investigate these proceedings and other Sixth Amendment rights in more detail."

DEVELOPMENT   1. For Activity 1 the students were to explain the key rights guaranteed under the Sixth Amendment.

2. Use the following questions to help focus the discussion:
   a. What does a speedy trial mean? What factors are involved?
   b. What is meant by a public trial?
   c. What is meant by a trial by an impartial jury?
   d. Does a person have the right to hear the specific charges in an indictment? Why or why not?
   e. What is meant by the right of confrontation?
   f. What is meant by compulsory process?
   g. What is meant by the right to counsel?

3. Discuss students' answers to Activities 2 and 3 for Lesson
    Seven.

4. Distribute and discuss the assignment for Lesson Eight.

**STUDENT
ASSIGNMENT
FOR THE NEXT
LESSON**

Have the students read Lesson Eight (Judge for Yourself)
and do the Activity for Lesson Eight. You may want to make
this two assignments.

Suggested Answers

**ACTIVITY 1 FOR
LESSON SEVEN**

Defining Terms 1–6

1. speedy trial – this clause does not guarantee that a trial
    must be held within a certain time limit; it only requires that
    factors be examined to see if the defendant's rights were
    violated by any unnecessary delay. These factors are: length
    of delay, reason for any delay, any complaint by the defen-
    dant that she or he is being denied a speedy trial, or any
    prejudice to the defendant (such as the death or disappear-
    ance of a witness or lost evidence).

2. public trial – trials must be open to the news media and the
    general public unless special circumstances warrant a closed
    trial. In the event the judge orders a trial closed, s/he must
    give valid and specific reasons for doing so.

3. trial by an impartial jury – a person is entitled to a jury trial
    for any charge more serious than petty (i.e., an offense pun-
    ishable by a prison term of more than six months). This
    means that jurors must be selected who have not already
    made up their minds as to the guilt or innocence of the ac-
    cused, who are not privy to special information, and who are
    selected without regard to their race, ethnicity, or sex.

4. right to confrontation – this gives the defendant or his/her
    attorney the right to question and cross-examine any witness
    who testifies against him/her.

5. compulsory process – this means that the court can order
    anyone to come to court and testify or give evidence in a case.
    This is usually done by presenting that person with a court
    order known as a subpoena. Anyone who ignores this order
    can be arrested and prosecuted for contempt of court.

6. right to counsel – this means that anyone charged with a
    crime has a right to be represented by an attorney. If a per-

son cannot afford an attorney, the court must appoint one to represent that person. A person can also elect to defend him/herself if he or she makes a knowing and intelligent waiver of the right to counsel.

ACTIVITY 2 FOR LESSON SEVEN

Supreme Court Decisions

1. In *Williams v. Florida* the Supreme Court decided that the U.S. Constitution does not require that a jury be composed of 12 members.

2. In *Johnson v. Louisiana* the Supreme Court decided that it is not a violation of due process if a twelve-person state jury does not render a unanimous verdict.

3. In *Burch v. Louisiana* the Supreme Court decided that a verdict rendered by a six-person jury must be unanimous.

4. *Barker v. Wingo* was a case in which factors were set out to help determine whether an accused was being denied a speedy trial; for example, length of delay of a case, reason for the delay, and any prejudice to the defendant (the death or disappearance of a witness or the loss of evidence).

ACTIVITY 3 FOR LESSON SEVEN

Questions 1–3

1. All three cases are important to a fair and impartial jury. A person should not be arbitrarily excluded from a jury because of sex or race. If a person is excluded because of sex or race, confidence in the jury's verdict can be shaken or destroyed. One of the cherished principles of American justice is equal justice for all. Courts have concluded that exclusion from a jury because of sex or race hurts both the defendant and the excluded juror. *Taylor v. Louisiana* prohibits exclusion on the basis of sex. *Strauder v. West Virginia* prohibits exclusion on the basis of race.

   It is often said that one of the things essential to maintaining confidence in the criminal justice system is the appearance of justice as well as justice itself. When a person is tried for allegedly committing a crime, our system requires that there be a prosecution, a defense, and an impartial judge and jury to decide the issues presented. To insure the appearance as well as the reality of impartiality, there should be no contact between the witnesses for the prosecution or the defense, on the one hand, and the jury, on the other. The decision in *Turner v. Louisiana* is an effort to insure an impartial jury by prohibiting these kinds of contacts.

2. The Sixth Amendment guarantees the right to counsel. The Sixth Amendment, like almost all of the other rights guaranteed in the Bill of Rights, is binding on the states through the due process clause of the Fourteenth Amendment. Few would dispute that a defendant needs the assistance of counsel when being prosecuted for a crime by the state. The three cases mentioned overturned convictions which were obtained when the defendant had no counsel or counsel was inappropriately obtained. The three cases also show the expansion of the right to counsel by the Supreme Court. In *Powell v. Alabama*, the right to counsel in capital (possibility of death as a punishment) cases was required. In *Gideon v. Wainwright*, the right to counsel in felony (serious crime) cases was guaranteed. In *Argersinger v. Hamlin*, the right to counsel in all cases where jail was a possibility was guaranteed.

3. Although a person has the right to an attorney, there are those persons who want to represent themselves even though they have had no legal training and are not lawyers. The Supreme Court has said that as long as a defendant knowingly waives the right to counsel, that is, is aware of the problems and pitfalls of self-representation, s/he has a constitutional right to represent him/herself. Persons may differ as to whether they believe this right is good or bad. On the one hand, it is the defendant who is being prosecuted and who may go to jail. The defendant should, thus, decide if s/he wants an attorney to represent him/her. On the other hand, it appears that a defendant who is untrained in the law would be no match for a trained prosecutor.

LESSON EIGHT: JUDGE FOR YOURSELF

Teacher Preparation

READ / REVIEW   1. Student book — Lesson Eight and the Activity for Lesson Eight.

2. Teacher's manual — the Suggested Answers to the Activity for Lesson Eight.

MATERIALS   No materials are needed for homework. The first lesson of Chapter Four (The Eighth Amendment) will be done as an in-class assignment.

Classroom Procedure

TIME   1–2 class periods

OBJECTIVES   The students will be able to:

1. Apply what they have learned in this chapter to cases involving Fifth and Sixth Amendment issues.

2. Use critical thinking skills such as evaluating, comparing, analyzing, and inferring to make decisions about some cases.

MOTIVATION   Tell the students, "Today we are going to use the knowledge we have gained about the Fifth and Sixth Amendments to analyze and make judgments about some cases."

DEVELOPMENT   1. Use any of a variety of group situations in order to allow students opportunities to interact and share ideas about the cases.

2. Have each group then report its consensus to the total class and discuss any different ideas.

STUDENT ASSIGNMENT FOR THE NEXT LESSON   The next lesson is an in-class assignment.

Suggested Answers

Case 1: *Parker v. Gladden*, 385 U.S. 363 (1966)

The Supreme Court found that the statements violated the defendant's right to an impartial jury guaranteed by the Sixth and Fourteenth Amendments. It reversed the conviction.

Comment: A jury deciding a case should be influenced only by the evidence introduced in the courtroom. During a trial a jury is often instructed not to read or listen to anything in the news media about the case. When a jury deliberates, it should not be swayed by any outside influences. The bailiff's comments were entirely improper. At a hearing to determine the effect of the remarks on the jury, one juror testified to being influenced by the bailiff's comments. Since at least one juror was influenced by the comments, a judge hearing the appeal would be justified in voting to reverse the conviction. On the other hand, if no juror had testified to being influenced by the remark, a judge hearing the appeal could vote to affirm the conviction.

Case 2: *Burch v. Louisiana*, 441 U.S. 130 (1979)

In this case the Supreme Court determined that when a jury consists of six persons, there must be a unanimous verdict or the right to trial by jury is violated.

Comment: A strong reason why a unanimous vote would be preferable to a 5 to 1 vote is the fact that when a vote is unanimous, all of the jurors hearing the case have agreed that the evidence is sufficient to convict. This lessens the chance that an error has been made. On the other hand, it can be argued that a 5 to 1 vote is still strong support for any verdict.

Case 3: *Lee v. Illinois*, 476 U.S. 530 (1986)

The Supreme Court reversed the conviction. It held that the judge's consideration of Thomas' confession (which stated that Lee and Thomas had planned the murders) violated the Confrontation Clause of the Sixth and Fourteenth Amendments.

Comment: In this case the judge considered the written confession of Thomas, which implicated Lee, in determining Lee's guilt. Since Thomas did not take the stand, the defense attorney for Lee never had a chance to question Thomas about his confession and about why Lee was implicated. This appears to be a clear violation of Lee's right to confront and cross-examine the witnesses against her. Thus it is a violation of the Sixth and Fourteenth Amendments.

Case 4: *Bruton v. United States*, 391 U.S. 123 (1968)

The Supreme Court reversed the conviction. It held that the introduction of the confession which implicated the second defendant violated his right to confront the witness against him.

Comment: The *Bruton* case is similar to *Lee v. Illinois*, above, in that a defense attorney did not have an opportunity to question a defendant who confessed and implicated another defendant. As in *Lee*, the right to confront a witness has been violated.

Case 5: *Escobedo v. Illinois*, 378 U.S. 478 (1964)

The Supreme Court reversed the conviction and suppressed the confession because of the failure to permit Escobedo to talk to his attorney.

Comment: This case was decided before *Miranda v. Arizona*. Today *Miranda* would require that the defendant be given Miranda warnings and that all questioning cease if the defendant asked for an attorney.

Case 6: *Brewer v. Williams*, 430 U.S. 387 (1977)

The Supreme Court ruled that the introduction of Williams' statements into evidence violated his right to counsel under the Sixth and Fourteenth Amendments. It reversed his conviction. Subsequently, Williams was retried, found guilty, and his conviction affirmed.

Comment: Williams' attorney had specifically instructed the police not to discuss the case with Williams on the road to Des Moines. The comments of the police officer to Williams, according to the majority decision, violated that request. Since his counsel was not present in the car, Williams' right to counsel was violated. If this view is taken, Williams' conviction should be reversed.

On the other hand, as the dissenters in the Supreme Court contended, there is an argument that Williams knew he had the right to have an attorney present and simply waived that right, volunteering to lead the police to the place where he had placed the body of the girl.

In fact, the Supreme Court of the United States reversed the conviction and ordered a new trial from which the defendant's statements were excluded. At the new trial, Williams was again convicted and the conviction was ultimately upheld by the Supreme Court in *Nix v. Williams*, 467 U.S. 431 (1984).

CHAPTER FOUR: THE EIGHTH AMENDMENT
LESSON ONE: YOU BE THE JUDGE

Teacher Preparation

READ / REVIEW

1. Student book — Lesson One and the Activity for Lesson One. Also read Lesson Four B where further comments are made concerning Case 1: *Wilkerson v. Utah.*

2. Teacher's manual — the Suggested Answers to the Activity for Lesson One.

MATERIALS

Student book — make copies of Lesson One and the Activity for Lesson One for use during this class period. Also make copies of Lesson Two (What Does the Eighth Amendment Say?) and the Activity for Lesson Two to distribute at the end of class.

Classroom Procedure

TIME

1 class period

OBJECTIVES

The students will be able to:

1. Analyze two cases relating to the Eighth Amendment and give their opinions about cruel and unusual punishment.

2. Determine whether a change in the conditions of a case alters their opinions about whether a punishment is cruel and unusual.

MOTIVATION

Tell the students, "Today we are going to look at two cases involving the Eighth Amendment and try to decide whether certain types of punishment in these cases are cruel and unusual. We'll learn more about the meaning of cruel and unusual punishment as we move further along in the chapter."

DEVELOPMENT

1. Ask the students, "What do you think the expression *cruel and unusual punishment* means?" Allow several students to give their opinions.

2. Divide the students into groups of 5 or 6 and assign each group one of the two cases in Lesson One.

3. Give each group a copy of the Guide for Analyzing Cases to fill out for their assigned case and ask them to appoint one of their members to record the group's answers.

4. After students have discussed the cases and filled out their Guide, they should come back together as a large group to discuss the cases and answer questions 1–4. Make certain that students discuss the reasoning behind their answers.

5. Distribute and discuss the assignment for Lesson Two.

STUDENT ASSIGNMENT FOR THE NEXT LESSON

Have the students read Lesson Two (What Does the Eighth Amendment Say?) and do the Activity for Lesson Two.

Suggested Answers

ACTIVITY FOR LESSON ONE

Wilkerson v. Utah, 99 U.S. 130 (1878) – Guide for Analyzing Cases

1. The main facts of the case are:
   a. Wilkerson was convicted of the murder of another person in the (then) Territory of Utah.
   b. He was sentenced to die by a firing squad.
   c. The Supreme Court of the Territory of Utah affirmed his sentence.
   d. The case went to the Supreme Court of the United States.
   e. There Wilkerson argued that it was cruel and unusual punishment to kill him by a firing squad.

2. The amendment involved was the Eighth Amendment.

3. Information not given. (The Cruel and Unusual Punishment Clause was involved.)

4. A territorial statute prohibited murder.

5. The issue was whether death by a firing squad was cruel and unusual punishment.

6. Information not given. (The Supreme Court affirmed the defendant's sentence of death by a firing squad.)

7. Information not given. (The Supreme Court ruled that there was no cruel and unusual punishment in death by a firing squad. There was no unnecessary or wanton infliction of pain as there would be in disemboweling, beheading, dissecting, or burning alive.)

Answer to Question 1 — *Wilkerson v. Utah*:
The issue here is not whether the infliction of the death penalty itself is cruel and unusual punishment. Many would argue that it is. The issue here is how the death penalty might be inflicted. One of the standards used by the Supreme Court in making this determination was whether there was unnecessary and wanton infliction of pain (see Lesson Four B).

Robinson v. California, 370 U.S. 660 (1962) – Guide for Analyzing Cases

1. The main facts of the case are:
   a. A police officer examined Robinson's arms and observed what appeared to be "needle marks" and a "scab" on the left arm and "scar tissue" and "discoloration" on the right arm.
   b. Robinson, was arrested for violating a California statute which made it a crime to be addicted to narcotics.
   c. Robinson was found guilty of violating the statute and sentenced to prison.
   d. His conviction was affirmed by the Appellate Department of the Los Angeles County Superior Court.
   e. Robinson then asked the Supreme Court of the United States to review his conviction.
   f. He argued that drug addiction was an illness, not a crime, and that to punish him for being an addict was cruel and unusual punishment which violated the Eighth and Fourteenth Amendments of the Constitution.

2. The amendment involved was the Eighth Amendment.

3. Information not given. (The Cruel and Unusual Punishment Clause was involved.)

4. The state statute violated was one that made it a crime to be addicted to narcotics.

5. The issue was whether the California statute making it a crime to be addicted to narcotics violated the Cruel and Unusual Punishment Clause of the Eighth Amendment.

6. Information not given. (The Supreme Court vacated [voided] Robinson's sentence.)

7. Information not given. (The Supreme Court ruled that it was cruel and unusual punishment to jail a person for being an addict. It stated that being an addict was a disease similar to being mentally ill, a leper, or having a venereal disease and, therefore, could not be criminally punished. The court noted,

however, that a person who sold or possessed narcotics within the state might be criminally prosecuted even if the seller or possessor were an addict.)

Answer to Questions 2–4 — *Robinson v. California*:
One of the arguments against jailing a person for drug addiction is that the craving for drugs by an addict is beyond the normal reasoning powers of a person; therefore, a drug addict should not be treated like a criminal. Rather, it is argued, a drug addiction should be treated as an illness rather than a crime. Note, however, that any crimes which an addict commits are still punishable under the law.

LESSON TWO: WHAT DOES THE EIGHTH AMENDMENT SAY?

Teacher Preparation

READ / REVIEW   1. Student book — Lesson Two and the Activity for Lesson Two.

2. Teacher's manual — the Suggested Answers to the Activity for Lesson Two.

MATERIALS   Student book — make copies of Lesson Three (What Are the Origins of the Eighth Amendment?) and the Activity for Lesson Three to distribute at the end of class.

Classroom Procedure

TIME   1 class period

OBJECTIVES   The students will be able to:

1. State what they believe the words of the Eighth Amendment mean.

2. Identify and explain what rights the Eighth Amendment grants.

MOTIVATION   Tell the students, "In this lesson we are going to examine the wording of the Eighth Amendment and identify which of our rights it guarantees."

DEVELOPMENT   1. Give several students the opportunity to share the words or phrases they chose to substitute for the words of the amendment. Make certain that students understand all of the vocabulary.

2. Have one student read his/her interpretation of the amendment. If other students have different interpretations, ask them to read theirs and to explain the ways in which their interpretations differ from others.

3. Ask the students to identify the rights guaranteed by the Eighth Amendment.

4. Distribute and discuss the assignment for Lesson Three.

STUDENT ASSIGNMENT FOR THE NEXT LESSON

Have the students read Lesson Three and do the Activity for Lesson Three.

Suggested Answers

ACTIVITY FOR LESSON TWO

Below are the most appropriate choices from the three alternatives provided. Be prepared to accept students' other choices as long as they are able to support their choices.

1. unnecessarily high
2. a sum of money required of a defendant to insure his/her return to court
3. ordered
4. sums of money which judges may order defendants who are found guilty to pay
5. ordered or directed
6. painful or hurtful
7. out of the ordinary
8. carried out

LESSON THREE: WHAT ARE THE ORIGINS OF THE EIGHTH AMENDMENT?

Teacher Preparation

READ / REVIEW   1. Student book — Lesson Three and the Activity for Lesson Three.

2. Teacher's manual — the Suggested Answers to the Activity for Lesson Three

MATERIALS   Student book — make copies of Lesson Four (The Eighth Amendment Today) and Activities 1–3 for Lesson Four to distribute at the end of class.

Classroom Procedure

TIME   1 class period

OBJECTIVES   The students will be able to:

1. Explain how certain cases and documents in English history helped establish the right to bail or the right to bail that was not excessive.

2. Explain why the Bill of Rights includes a provision against cruel and unusual punishment.

MOTIVATION   Tell the students, "As we learned in the Fourth Amendment chapter, Magna Carta had an important influence on the Bill of Rights. Today we will discuss how this and other English documents, as well as two famous historical cases, influenced the Eighth Amendment."

DEVELOPMENT   1. Recall the history of Magna Carta and the influence the English had on the American Colonies (from Chapter Two).

2. Read each question in the Activity for Lesson Three and have the students share their answers. Discuss any disagreements among the answers, making certain that students support their reasoning.

3. Distribute and discuss the materials for Lesson Four.

STUDENT ASSIGNMENT FOR THE NEXT LESSON

Have the students do Activities 1–3 for Lesson Four. These activities are rather extensive and you will probably want to make this two or three assignments.

Suggested Answers

ACTIVITY FOR LESSON THREE

Questions 1–3

1. Cases and documents which helped establish the right to bail or the right against excessive bail:

   Darnel's Case — The controversy surrounding *Darnel's Case* gave rise to Parliament's passage of the Petition of Right in 1628. The Petition of Right provided that people like Darnel who had been arrested and were awaiting trial should be given bail.

   Jenkes's Case — Jenkes's detention in jail for approximately two months was one reason why the Habeas Corpus Act of 1679 was passed in England. In part, the Act made it possible for persons who claimed that they were being held in jail for reasons such as high bail to have the issue resolved by the court quickly.

   Magna Carta — Magna Carta contained a provision that a person should not be arrested or detained in jail unless the law of the land so provided. Magna Carta was invoked by the knights in *Darnel's Case* as a document which guaranteed them due process.

   Petition of Right of 1628 — The Petition of Right made it possible for persons to be given bail while they were awaiting trial.

   English Bill of Rights of 1689 — This document specifically included a provision prohibiting excessive bail.

2. The framers of the Constitution included a provision against cruel and unusual punishment as part of the Eighth Amendment to prevent the possibility of torture and physically harmful punishments like those that had been practiced in England.

3. Prior to the U.S. Bill of Rights, the issue of cruel and unusual punishment was addressed in Magna Carta, the Petition of Right of 1628, and the English Bill of Rights of 1689.

LESSON FOUR: THE EIGHTH AMENDMENT TODAY

Teacher Preparation

READ / REVIEW   1. Student book — Lesson Four and Activities 1–3 for Lesson Four.

2. Teacher's manual — the Suggested Answers to Activities 1–3 for Lesson Four.

MATERIALS   Student book — make copies of Lesson Five (Judge for Yourself) and the Activity for Lesson Five to distribute at the end of class.

Classroom Procedure

TIME   2–3 class periods

OBJECTIVES   The students will be able to:

1. Explain the purpose of bail, identify factors a judge uses in setting bail, and define excessive bail.

2. State the standards for determining whether a punishment is cruel and unusual.

3. Debate the arguments for and against the death penalty.

MOTIVATION   Ask the students, "How many of you favor the death penalty? How many think it is cruel and unusual punishment?" Take a quick count for comparison with students' views later in the lesson, then tell them, "In this lesson, we will discuss how the issues of cruel and unusual punishment are viewed by the Supreme Court today."

DEVELOPMENT   1. Lesson Four consists of parts A, B, and C. Use the questions in Activities 1–3 to stimulate class discussion of the topics in these sections.

2. Lesson Four A deals with excessive bail. Have the students identify and discuss the factors judges consider when setting bail.

3. Lesson Four B deals with cruel and unusual punishment. Have the students state and discuss the standards for determining whether a punishment is cruel and unusual.

4. Lesson Four C deals with the death penalty. Two cases are cited: one that outlawed the death penalty and one that stated that the death penalty could be used. The students can divide into groups and discuss the arguments for and against the death penalty. Teams can be established and the students can debate the issue, arguing for one position or the other.

   It should be noted that the death penalty continues to be controversial in America. Some states still oppose it even though the Supreme Court has said it is not a violation of the Eighth and Fourteenth Amendments to the Constitution.

5. After their discussion, poll students again about their view on the death penalty. Note whether any students have changed their opinions since the beginning of the lesson.

6. Have the students select cases from their case notebooks and tell what bail they think should be required in each case. Also have them state what punishment they believe would be appropriate for the crime committed.

7. Distribute and discuss the materials for Lesson Five.

STUDENT ASSIGNMENT FOR THE NEXT LESSON

Have the students read Lesson Five and do the Activity for Lesson Five. Remind the students that when answering the questions for this activity, their decisions as judges may not necessarily agree with their personal opinions.

Suggested Answers

ACTIVITY 1 FOR LESSON FOUR

Questions 1–6

1. Bail is an amount of money, set by a judge, that a defendant must pay in order to be released from jail while awaiting trial.

2. Excessive bail is an amount set so high that a defendant cannot possibly pay it.

3. Being released on one's own recognizance means that a person is released without having to pay bail. This happens when a judge decides that the person can be relied upon to appear for trial. The judge's decision is based upon the defendant's previous record of reliability and position in and ties to the community.

4. A judge will consider the kind of crime involved, the defendant's previous record, whether a defendant has failed

to return to court before, and the ties a defendant has to the community.

Other factors might be the defendant's ability to raise bail, the length of time the defendant might have to spend in jail until the trial date, and the severity of the sentence if the defendant is found guilty.

5. This question simply calls for students' opinions.

6. In *Stack v. Boyle* the Supreme Court decided that the purpose of bail was to insure that a defendant would return to court without having to remain in jail while awaiting trial.

ACTIVITY 2 FOR LESSON FOUR

Questions 1–8

1. Yes. The case of *Robinson v. California* stated that the Eighth Amendment's provision on cruel and unusual punishments applies to the states.

2. The two standards are that the punishment must not involve unnecessary or wanton (malicious) infliction of pain and that the punishment must not be out of proportion to the crime committed.

3. Four types of punishment considered unusually cruel by the Supreme Court are disemboweling, beheading, burning alive, and dragging to the place of execution.

4. The Supreme Court decided in *Wilkerson v. Utah* that being executed by a firing squad is not cruel and unusual punishment. Students should give their opinions about whether they agree or disagree with the decision and state their reasons.

5. Punishment out of proportion to the crime means that the punishment is far too severe for the type or degree of crime committed.

6. In *Solem v. Helm* the Supreme Court found that Helm's sentence of life in prison without possibility of parole was out of proportion to the crime of writing a bad check for $100. Their reasoning was that all of his crimes were relatively minor, an appeals court had already found his sentence cruel and unusual, he had been treated more harshly than other criminals in the state who had committed similar crimes, and his punishment was more harsh than it would have been in almost every other state.

7. This question asks for students' opinions, but certain guidelines might be applied to their reasoning. On the one hand, it can be argued that the defendant's crimes were relatively

minor, that none involved violence to another person, that they occurred after the defendant had taken alcohol, and that other persons who had committed more serious crimes had received lesser penalties. On the other hand, it can be argued that the defendant had repeatedly violated the law and apparently showed little possibility of rehabilitation.

8. This question simply calls for the students' opinions.

ACTIVITY 3 FOR LESSON FOUR

Questions 1–5

1. In *Furman v. Georgia* the Supreme Court outlawed the death penalty in America as it was then being applied. Two justices considered it cruel and unusual, period. Three justices felt it was just cruel and unusual in the way it was being applied at that time.

2. In *Gregg v. Georgia* the Supreme Court upheld the death penalty, saying that the Eighth and Fourteenth Amendments did not bar the death penalty, and that the death penalty was not cruel and unusual in all cases. Georgia had instituted a new procedure that required a trial to see if the death penalty should be imposed on a defendant and considered the defendant's past criminal record and the way the particular murder had been carried out.

3 and 4. These questions simply ask for the students' opinions. Ask students to give the reasoning behind their opinions.

5. The students can give their own opinions about whether or not the death penalty should be imposed. Their reasons may or may not include the reasons for and against the death penalty listed in Lesson Four C.

LESSON FIVE: JUDGE FOR YOURSELF

Teacher Preparation

READ / REVIEW
1. Student book — Lesson Five and the Activity for Lesson Five.
2. Teacher's manual — the Suggested Answers to the Activity for Lesson Five.

MATERIALS
No materials are needed for homework. The first lesson of Chapter Five (The Second, Third, and Seventh Amendments) will be done as an in-class activity.

Classroom Procedure

TIME
1–2 class periods

OBJECTIVES
The students will be able to:
1. Apply what they have learned from previous lessons in this chapter to cases involving Eighth Amendment issues.
2. Use critical thinking skills such as evaluating, analyzing, and inferring to make decisions about some cases.

MOTIVATION
Tell the students, "Today we are going to use what we have learned about the Eighth Amendment to judge several cases for ourselves."

DEVELOPMENT
1. Use a variety of group situations in order to allow students opportunities to interact and share ideas about the cases.
2. Students' answers to the case questions can be shared with the whole class.

STUDENT ASSIGNMENT FOR THE NEXT LESSON
The next lesson is an in-class assignment.

Suggested Answers

ACTIVITY FOR LESSON FIVE

Case 1: *Rummel v. Estelle*, 445 U.S. 263 (1980)

The Supreme Court held that the sentence did not violate the provision against cruel and unusual punishment. It stated that Texas had an interest in treating repeat offenders more harshly than other offenders and that a court should be reluctant to change a sentence authorized by the legislature. The Court also noted that there was a possibility of parole. Subsequently, the legislature passed a law stating that crimes such as those committed by the defendant could be punished only for a maximum of ten years. (See *Hutto v. Davis*, 454 U.S. 370, 379 concurring opinion of Justice Powell.)

Comment: The arguments on both sides in *Rummel v. Estelle* can be similar to those made in *Solem v. Helm*. On the one hand, the crimes were relatively minor. On the other hand, the defendant was a repeat offender. The issue is whether the sentence is out of proportion to the crime committed. (See Lesson Four B.)

Case 2: *Hutto v. Davis*, 454 U.S. 370 (1982)

The Supreme Court of the United States held that the sentence did not violate the Eighth and Fourteenth Amendments.

Comment: The Supreme Court in *Hutto* said that the decision in *Rummel v. Estelle* controlled (was precedent for) the decision it was making. It concluded that the legislature had determined by statute the minimum and maximum sentences. Therefore, any change in the statute determining the length of a sentence should come from the legislature. A sentence within the limits set by the legislature should normally not be considered cruel and unusual.

Case 3: *Louisiana ex rel. Francis v. Resweber*, 329 U.S. 459 (1947)

The Supreme Court of the United States held that it was not cruel and unusual punishment to place the defendant in the electric chair a second time.

Comment: In this case, the fact that the electric chair malfunctioned did not change the fact that the defendant had murdered another person and had been sentenced to death for that crime.

Case 4: *Coker v. Georgia*, 433 U.S. 584 (1977)

The Supreme Court of the United States held that it was cruel and unusual punishment to impose the death sentence for rape.

Comment: In *Coker v. Georgia*, the Supreme Court set a limit on the type of crime for which death might be imposed. The question as to whether the death penalty should be imposed in instances other than murder is one on which opinions differ.

Case 5: *Enmund v. Florida*, 458 U.S. 782 (1982)

The Supreme Court reversed the sentence. It noted that Enmund did not kill or intend to kill the two persons. Therefore, the sentence of death was a violation of the Eighth and Fourteenth Amendments.

Comment: In *Enmund v. Florida* the Supreme Court placed a further limit on the imposition of the death penalty finding it could not be imposed on a person who had not directly participated in the crime.

CHAPTER FIVE: THE SECOND, THIRD, & SEVENTH AMENDMENTS

LESSON ONE: YOU BE THE JUDGE – THE SECOND AMENDMENT

Teacher Preparation

READ / REVIEW
1. Student book — Lesson One and the Activity for Lesson One.
2. Teacher's manual — the Suggested Answers to the Activity for Lesson One.

MATERIALS
Student book — make copies of Lesson One and the Activity for Lesson One for use during this class period. Also make copies of Lesson Two (What Does the Second Amendment Say?) and the Activity for Lesson Two to distribute at the end of class.

Classroom Procedure

TIME
1 class period

OBJECTIVES
The students will be able to:
1. Analyze two cases relating to the Second Amendment.
2. Give their opinions about people's right to carry and transport firearms.

MOTIVATION
Tell the students, "Today we are going to look at two cases involving the Second Amendment and discuss issues involving the private ownership of guns."

DEVELOPMENT
1. Ask the students, "Who do you think should be able to keep a gun?" Allow several students to give their opinions.
2. Now divide the students into groups of 5 or 6 and assign each group one of the two cases in Lesson One.
3. Give each group a copy of the Guide for Analyzing Cases to fill out for their assigned case and ask them to appoint one member of their group to record the group's answers.
4. After the students have discussed the cases and filled out

their Guides, have them come back together as a large group to share their analyses and discuss questions 1 and 2. Make certain that students discuss the reasons for their answers.

5. Distribute and discuss the assignment for Lesson Two.

STUDENT ASSIGNMENT FOR THE NEXT LESSON

Have the students read Lesson Two (What Does the Second Amendment Say?) and do the Activity for Lesson Two.

Suggested Answers

ACTIVITY FOR LESSON ONE

Presser v. Illinois, **116 U.S. 252 (1886) – Guide for Analyzing Cases**

1. The main facts of the case are:
    a. In 1879 in Illinois, Herman Presser belonged to an organization which engaged in military exercises as one of its functions.
    b. Along with other members of the organization, Presser paraded through the streets of Chicago carrying a gun.
    c. Presser was arrested for violating an Illinois law which prohibited persons who were not members of the state militia from parading with guns without a license from the governor.
    d. Presser was convicted and fined ten dollars.
    e. He appealed to the Illinois Supreme Court which affirmed his conviction.
    f. Presser then took his case to the Supreme Court of the United States where he argued, among other things, that the Illinois statute violated his right to bear arms guaranteed by the Second Amendment.

2. The amendment involved was the Second Amendment.

3. Information not given. (The whole amendment was involved including the clause referring to a militia and one granting to citizens the right to bear arms.)

4. An Illinois statute prohibited persons who were not members of the state militia from carrying guns in a parade without a license from the governor.

5. The issue was whether the Illinois statute violated Presser's right to bear arms guaranteed by the Second Amendment.

6. Information not given. (The Supreme Court ruled that the Second Amendment was not violated by the Illinois statute [see Lesson Three].)

7. Information not given. (The Supreme Court held that there was no violation of the right to bear arms. It also ruled that the Second Amendment applied only to the federal government and not to the state governments.)

Question 1 — *Presser v. Illinois*:
This question calls for students' opinions.

United States v. Miller, 307 U.S. 175 (1939) – Guide for Analyzing Cases

1. The main facts of the case are:
   a. Jack Miller and another person were indicted for transporting an unregistered shotgun in interstate commerce in violation of the National Firearms Act of 1934.
   b. The Act required that such firearms be registered with the Internal Revenue Service and that the owner have a stamped order.

2. The amendment involved was the Second Amendment.

3. Information not given. (The entire amendment was involved including the clause referring to a militia and one granting to citizens the right to bear arms.)

4. The National Firearms Act of 1934 (a federal statute) was involved.

5. The issue was whether the National Firearms Act was a violation of the Second Amendment.

6. Information not given. (The Supreme Court ruled that there was no violation of the Second Amendment [see Lesson Three].)

7. Information not given. (The Supreme Court stated that the purpose of the amendment was to preserve a militia; thus, the National Firearms Act did not violate the Second Amendment.)

Question 2 — *United States v. Miller*:
This question calls for students' opinions.

LESSON TWO: WHAT DOES THE SECOND AMENDMENT SAY?

Teacher Preparation

READ / REVIEW   1. Student book — Lesson Two and the Activity for Lesson Two.

2. Teacher's manual — the Suggested Answers to the Activity for Lesson Two.

MATERIALS   Student book — make copies of Lesson Three (What Is the Purpose of the Second Amendment?) and the Activity for Lesson Three to distribute at the end of class.

Classroom Procedure

TIME   1 class period

OBJECTIVES   The students will be able to:

1. State what they believe the words of the Second Amendment mean.

2. Identify and explain what rights the Second Amendment grants.

MOTIVATION   Tell the students, "In this lesson we are going to examine the wording of the Second Amendment and identify which of our rights it guarantees."

DEVELOPMENT   1. Give several students the opportunity to share the words or phrases they chose to substitute for the words of the amendment. Make certain that students understand all of the vocabulary.

2. Have one student read his/her interpretation of the amendment. If other students have different interpretations, ask them to explain how and why theirs differ.

3. Distribute and discuss the assignment for Lesson Three.

STUDENT ASSIGNMENT FOR THE NEXT LESSON   Have the students read Lesson Three (What Is the Purpose of the Second Amendment?) and do the Activity for Lesson Three.

Suggested Answers

ACTIVITY FOR LESSON TWO   Below are the most appropriate choices from the three alternatives provided. Be prepared to accept students' other choices as long as they are able to support their choices.

1. controlled
2. private citizens who can be called to duty in an emergency
3. safety
4. citizens
5. carry
6. hindered

Lesson Three: WHAT IS THE PURPOSE OF THE SECOND AMENDMENT?

Teacher Preparation

READ / REVIEW
1. Student book — Lesson Three and the Activity for Lesson Three.

2. Teacher's manual — the Suggested Answers to the Activity for Lesson Three

MATERIALS
Student book — make copies of Lesson Four (You Be the Judge – The Third Amendment) and the Activity for Lesson Four to distribute at the end of class.

Classroom Procedure

TIME
1 class period

OBJECTIVES
The students will be able to:

1. Discuss the purpose of the Second Amendment.

2. State whether they agree or disagree with the Supreme Court's decisions in *Presser v. Illinois* and *United States v. Miller* and discuss their reasons.

MOTIVATION
Tell the students, "Gun control is a major concern in our society today. We will return to the two cases from Lesson One to help us in our discussion of this controversial issue."

DEVELOPMENT
1. Ask a student to share his/her summary of the purpose of the Second Amendment.

2. Ask another student to relate the Supreme Court's decisions in *Presser v. Illinois* and *United States v. Miller*.

3. Have several students state whether they agree or disagree with the decisions in these cases. Make certain that the students support their reasoning.

4. Let the students debate any disagreements among their answers.

5. Distribute and discuss the assignment for Lesson Four.

STUDENT ASSIGNMENT FOR THE NEXT LESSON

Have the students read Lesson Four (You Be the Judge – The Third Amendment) and do the Activity for Lesson Four.

Suggested Answers

ACTIVITY FOR LESSON THREE

Questions 1–3

1. The purpose of the Second Amendment was to prevent the federal government from keeping a standing army in peace-time. The Founding Fathers felt that a standing army might be used to support a tyrannical government. They believed that a militia—a body of private citizens who could be called to duty only during emergencies—would cause a government to hesitate before it imposed tyrannical rule.

2. The Supreme Court upheld Presser's conviction and rejected the argument that the Second Amendment was violated. It stated that the Illinois statute that required groups to have a permit in order to parade with guns did not infringe on any right to keep and bear arms. It also stated that the Second Amendment was binding only on the federal government, not the state governments. The second part of this question calls for students' opinions.

3. The Supreme Court upheld Miller's conviction. It stated that the National Firearms Act did not violate the Second Amendment. It noted that the purpose of the Second Amendment was to provide for a militia. The second part of this question calls for students' opinions.

LESSON FOUR: YOU BE THE JUDGE – THE THIRD AMENDMENT

Teacher Preparation

READ / REVIEW   1. Student book — Lesson Four and the Activity for Lesson Four.

2. Teacher's manual — the Suggested Answers to the Activity for Lesson Four.

MATERIALS   Student book — make copies of Lesson Five (What Does the Third Amendment Say?) and the Activity for Lesson Five to distribute at the end of class.

Classroom Procedure

TIME   1 class period

OBJECTIVES   The students will be able to:

1. Analyze a case related to the Third Amendment.

2. Give their opinions about whether or not housing soldiers in correctional officers' quarters at a correctional facility violated the officers' Third Amendment rights.

MOTIVATION   Tell the students, "Today we will examine a case involving the Third Amendment and decide whether anyone's rights were violated in this case."

DEVELOPMENT   1. Divide the students into groups of 5 or 6 and have each group discuss the case in Lesson Four.

2. Give each group a copy of the Guide for Analyzing Cases to fill out for the case and ask them to appoint one member of their group to record the group's answers.

3. After the students have discussed the case and filled out their Guides, have them come back together as a large group to share their analyses and discuss the question following the case. Make certain that students discuss the reasons for their answers.

4. Distribute and discuss the assignment for Lesson Five.

STUDENT ASSIGNMENT FOR THE NEXT LESSON

Have the students read Lesson Five (What Does the Third Amendment Say?) and do the Activity for Lesson Five.

Suggested Answers

ACTIVITY FOR LESSON FOUR

Engblom v. Carey, **522 Federal Supplement 57 (United States District Court Southern District of New York, 1981) – Guide for Analyzing Cases**
1. The main facts of the case are:
   a. A strike of correctional officers (prison guards) occurred in New York State.
   b. During the strike, some of the officers who lived in the Mid-Orange Correctional Facility were barred from their homes at the correctional facility and National Guardsmen were housed there.
   c. After the strike was over, the correctional officers claimed that their rights under the Third Amendment were violated. They sued for money damages.
2. The Third Amendment was involved.
3. The entire Amendment was involved.
4. No state or federal statute was involved.
5. The issue was whether the Third Amendment was violated by housing the National Guardsmen in the residences of the correctional officers.
6. Information not given. (The case never reached the Supreme Court. The federal district court ruled that the Third Amendment was not violated [see Lesson Six].)
7. Information not given. (The federal district court said that no clearly established constitutional right was involved because the officials of the correctional facility had no way of knowing, by past decisions or otherwise, that they would violate the Third Amendment by removing the officers from their homes.)

Question following case – *Engblom v. Carey*
This question asks only for students' opinions.

LESSON FIVE: WHAT DOES THE THIRD AMENDMENT SAY?

Teacher Preparation

READ / REVIEW
1. Student book — Lesson Five and the Activity for Lesson Five.

2. Teacher's manual — the Suggested Answers to the Activity for Lesson Five.

MATERIALS
Student book — make copies of Lesson Six (What is the Purpose of the Third Amendment?) and the Activity for Lesson Six to distribute at the end of class.

Classroom Procedure

TIME
1 class period

OBJECTIVES
The students will be able to:

1. State what they believe the words of the Third Amendment mean.

2. Identify and explain what rights the Third Amendment grants.

MOTIVATION
Tell the students, "In this lesson we are going to examine the wording of the Third Amendment and identify which of our rights it guarantees."

DEVELOPMENT
1. Give several students the opportunity to share the words or phrases they chose to substitute for the words of the amendment. Make certain that students understand all of the vocabulary.

2. Have one student read his/her interpretation of the amendment. If other students have different interpretations, ask them to explain how and why theirs differ.

3. Distribute and discuss the assignment for Lesson Six.

STUDENT ASSIGNMENT FOR THE NEXT LESSON

Have the students read Lesson Six (What Is the Purpose of the Third Amendment?) and do the Activity for Lesson Six.

Suggested Answers

ACTIVITY FOR LESSON FIVE

Below are the most appropriate choices from the three alternatives provided. Be prepared to accept students' other choices as long as they are able to support their choices.

1. lodged
2. agreement
3. way
4. directed or set out

Lesson Six: WHAT IS THE PURPOSE OF THE THIRD AMENDMENT?

Teacher Preparation

READ / REVIEW

1. Student book — Lesson Six and the Activity for Lesson Six.

2. Teacher's manual — the Suggested Answers to the Activity for Lesson Six.

MATERIALS

Student book — make copies of Lesson Seven (You Be the Judge – The Seventh Amendment) and the Activity for Lesson Seven to distribute at the end of class.

Classroom Procedure

TIME

1 class period

OBJECTIVES

The students will be able to:

1. Discuss the purpose of the Third Amendment.

2. State the decision in *Engblom v. Carey* and discuss whether they agree or disagree with the decision of the federal district court.

3. Express their points of view regarding whether or not, and under what circumstances, troops could be quartered in a private home.

4. State their opinions about the need for the Third Amendment today.

MOTIVATION

Tell the students, "Today we will discuss the purpose of the Third Amendment and try to determine how, and whether, it should be applied in our time."

DEVELOPMENT

1. Ask a student to share his/her summary of the purpose of the Third Amendment.

2. Ask another student to relate the decision of the court in *Engblom v. Carey*.

3. Have several students state whether they agree or disagree

with the decision of the court in this case. Make certain that the students support their reasoning.

4. Give several students the opportunity to state, as judges, if and when they would permit troops to be quartered in private residences.

5. Ask the students, "Do you believe there is a need for the Third Amendment today?" Let the students debate this question in small groups or as a whole class.

6. Distribute and discuss the assignment for Lesson Seven.

STUDENT ASSIGNMENT FOR THE NEXT LESSON

Have students do Lesson Seven (You Be the Judge – The Seventh Amendment) and the Activity for Lesson Seven.

=====

Suggested Answers

ACTIVITY FOR LESSON SIX

Questions 1–3

1. The purpose of the Third Amendment is to protect citizens from having to house soldiers in their homes in times of peace (and only under strict guidelines in times of war or other emergency).

2. In *Engblom v. Carey*, the Supreme Court stated that the Third Amendment was not binding on the states. The court ruled that the officials of the prison had no way of knowing, by past decisions or otherwise, that they would violate the Third Amendment by removing the officers from their homes and that they had not violated any statutory or constitutional rights "of which a reasonable person would have known." The second part of this question calls for students' opinions.

3. This question calls for students' opinions. Students should be able to devise scenarios in which housing soldiers in private homes would be unavoidable and also be able to create rules for doing so that would protect the citizens' rights and their possessions.

Lesson Seven: YOU BE THE JUDGE – THE SEVENTH AMENDMENT

Teacher Preparation

READ / REVIEW
1. Student book — Lesson Seven and the Activity for Lesson Seven.

2. Teacher's manual — the Suggested Answers to the Activity for Lesson Seven.

MATERIALS
Student book — make copies of Lesson Eight (What Does the Seventh Amendment Say?) and the Activity for Lesson Eight to distribute at the end of class.

Classroom Procedure

TIME
1 class period

OBJECTIVES
The students will be able to:

1. Analyze a case involving the Seventh Amendment.

2. Discuss whether there should be a jury trial in civil cases in which no jail sentence is involved.

MOTIVATION
Tell the students, "Today we are going to discuss a case involving a business corporation and the Seventh Amendment."

DEVELOPMENT
1. Divide the students into groups of 5 or 6 and assign each group the case in Lesson One.

2. Give each group a copy of the Guide for Analyzing Cases to fill out for the case and have them choose one member of their group to record the group's answers.

3. After the students have discussed the case and filled out their Guides, have them come back together as a large group to share their analyses and discuss the question following the case.

4. Distribute and discuss the assignment for Lesson Eight.

STUDENT ASSIGNMENT FOR THE NEXT LESSON

Have the students do Lesson Eight (What Does the Seventh Amendment Say?) and the Activity for Lesson Eight.

Suggested Answers

ACTIVITY FOR LESSON SEVEN

Ross v. Bernhard, 396 U.S. 531 (1970) – Guide for Analyzing Cases

1. The main facts of the case are:
   a. Stockholders brought what is known as a stockholders' derivative action against the officers and directors of a corporation.
   b. The suit was on behalf of the corporation and sought to require the officers and directors to give back to the corporation money claimed to have been wasted by the officers and directors.

2. The Amendment involved was the Seventh Amendment.

3. The entire Amendment and its requirement of a jury trial in certain cases was involved.

4. The state statute involved was one which permitted stockholders' derivative actions. In other words, the statute permitted stockholders to sue the officers and directors for money claimed to have been lost by the officers and directors.

5. The issue was whether the Seventh Amendment required a jury trial in this case (or cases like this).

6. Information not given. (The Supreme Court concluded that a jury trial was required [see Lesson Nine].)

7. Information not given. (The Supreme Court stated that, historically, if the corporation had brought the suit [a suit authorized by the directors], a jury trial would have been required. In the same fashion, a jury trial was required even though it was the shareholders who brought the suit on behalf of the corporation.)

Question following the case – *Ross v. Bernhard*
This question calls for students' opinions.

LESSON EIGHT: WHAT DOES THE SEVENTH AMENDMENT SAY?

Teacher Preparation

READ / REVIEW

1. Student book — Lesson Eight and the Activity for Lesson Eight.

2. Teacher's manual — the Suggested Answers to the Activity for Lesson Eight.

MATERIALS

Student book — make copies of Lesson Nine (What Is the Purpose of the Seventh Amendment?) and the Activity for Lesson Nine to distribute at the end of class.

Classroom Procedure

TIME

1 class period

OBJECTIVES

The students will be able to:

1. State what they believe the words of the Seventh Amendment mean.

2. Identify and explain what rights the Seventh Amendment grants.

MOTIVATION

Tell the students, "In this lesson we are going to examine the wording of the Seventh Amendment and identify which of our rights it guarantees."

DEVELOPMENT

1. Give several students the opportunity to share the words or phrases they chose to substitute for the words of the amendment. Make certain that students understand all of the vocabulary.

2. Have one student read his/her interpretation of the amendment. If other students have different interpretations, ask them to explain how and why theirs differ.

3. Distribute and discuss the assignment for Lesson Nine.

**STUDENT
ASSIGNMENT
FOR THE NEXT
LESSON**

Have students do Lesson Nine (What Is the Purpose of the Seventh Amendment?) and the Activity for Lesson Nine.

Suggested Answers

**ACTIVITY FOR
LESSON EIGHT**

Below are the most appropriate choices from the three alternatives provided. Be prepared to accept students' other choices as long as they are able to support their choices.

1. lawsuits
2. laws based on custom, common usage, and decisions judges have made in similar cases
3. amount of money
4. dispute
5. group of people chosen to decide a case
6. kept
7. issue in dispute
8. heard and decided
9. heard and decided a second time

LESSON NINE: WHAT IS THE PURPOSE OF THE SEVENTH AMENDMENT?

Teacher Preparation

READ / REVIEW   1. Student book — Lesson Nine and the Activity for Lesson Nine.

2. Teacher's manual — the Suggested Answers to the Activity for Lesson Nine.

MATERIALS   Student book — make copies of the Concluding Activity questions which follow Lesson Nine to distribute at the end of this class or at the beginning of the next class.

Classroom Procedure

TIME   1 class period

OBJECTIVES   The students will be able to:

1. Discuss the purpose of the Seventh Amendment.

2. Determine whether the Seventh Amendment is applicable to the states.

3. State the decision in *Ross v. Bernhard* and discuss whether they agree or disagree with the decision of the court.

MOTIVATION   Tell the students, "Today we will discuss the purpose and application of the Seventh Amendment."

DEVELOPMENT   1. Ask a student to share his/her summary of the purpose of the Seventh Amendment.

2. Ask another student to state whether the Seventh Amendment guarantees a right to a jury trial in civil cases in state courts. Make certain that the student gives his/her reasons.

3. Have one student relate the decision of the court in *Ross v. Bernhard*.

4. Have several students state whether they agree or disagree with the decision of the court in this case. Make certain that the students support their reasoning.

STUDENT ASSIGNMENT FOR THE NEXT LESSON

Either as homework or at the beginning of the next lesson, have the students read and reflect upon the Concluding Activity (Questions for Reflection) questions. They should be prepared for a whole class discussion of these final questions. Additional questions and extending activities are provided in the teacher's suggestions at the beginning of this manual.

Suggested Answers

ACTIVITY FOR LESSON NINE

Questions 1–3

1. The purpose of the Seventh Amendment is to insure that in certain civil cases, there is a right to a trial by jury.

2. The Seventh Amendment does not guarantee a right to a jury trial in civil cases in state courts. The Seventh Amendment is binding only on the federal government.

3. In *Ross v. Bernhard*, the Supreme Court decided that a jury trial was required because, historically, if the corporation had brought the suit [a suit authorized by the directors], a jury trial would have been required. In the same fashion, a jury trial was required even though it was the shareholders who brought the suit on behalf of the corporation. The second part of this question calls for students' opinions.

GUIDE FOR ANALYZING CASES

Case:

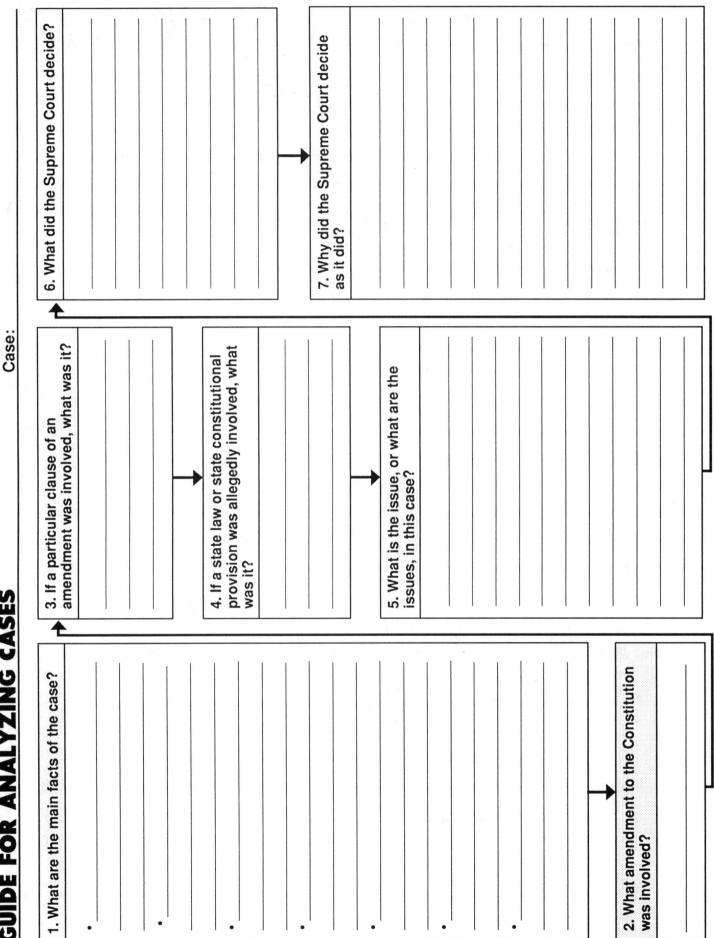

1. What are the main facts of the case?

2. What amendment to the Constitution was involved?

3. If a particular clause of an amendment was involved, what was it?

4. If a state law or state constitutional provision was allegedly involved, what was it?

5. What is the issue, or what are the issues, in this case?

6. What did the Supreme Court decide?

7. Why did the Supreme Court decide as it did?

EXTENDING ACTIVITIES

1. Explore the costs of our judicial system and debate whether it is worth the expenditure for general court costs, court appointed attorneys, costs of numerous appeals for convicted criminals, costs of incarcerations, and buildings to house our legal systems.

2. Debate the consequences of a lesser judicial system and suggestions for alternatives to the current system.

3. Explore the legal systems of other countries. Compare and contrast these systems with the U.S. legal system.

4. Compare and contrast the human rights struggle in the American colonies with the struggles of other countries trying to gain human rights and emancipation today.

5. Debate current legal issues: whether there should be a limit placed on appeals; the effectiveness of the death penalty; standardization of prison sentences; how to speed up the system and get rid of the backlog of cases; and additional topics of concern to students.

6. Debate what the qualifications for a judge should be including education, personal values, social and community attitudes, and experience.

7. Debate the best way for judges to gain their positions: appointed or elected; limited terms vs. life term; advantages and disadvantages for both sides of the argument.

8. Examine the Ninth and Tenth Amendments and determine whether or not they also have an application to human rights.

CONNECTIONS TO OTHER DISCIPLINES

1. Explore how gathering evidence for a criminal case relates to science and mathematics. Students can study what processes are used for ballistics reports, crime reports, and other forensic lab investigations.

2. Lessons can be connected to reading and English classes by having students read historical or suspense novels that show how legal procedures have been used in the fight for human justice.

3. Students can also read biographies of the writers of the Constitution and the Bill of Rights and report to the class about the difficulties these men encountered as they strived to accomplish human rights in their times.

4. Have students read biographies of other historical figures who struggled with human rights issues. Awareness of the depth and length of the ongoing struggle for equal rights for women and minority groups can motivate students to take greater interest in current events and provide a contemporary and concrete connection to social studies.